**New Directions for
Institutional Research**

Robert K. Toutkoushian
EDITOR-IN-CHIEF

J. Fredericks Volkwein
ASSOCIATE EDITOR

Alternative Perspectives in Institutional Planning

Terry T. Ishitani
EDITOR

Number 137 • Spring 2008
Jossey-Bass
San Francisco

ALTERNATIVE PERSPECTIVES IN INSTITUTION PLANNING
Terry T. Ishitani (ed.)
New Directions for Institutional Research, no. 137
Robert K. Toutkoushian, Editor-in-Chief

NEW DIRECTIONS FOR INSTITUTIONAL RESEARCH (ISSN 0271-0579, electronic ISSN 1536-075X) is part of The Jossey-Bass Higher and Adult Education Series and is published quarterly by Wiley Subscription Services, Inc., A Wiley Company, at Jossey-Bass, 989 Market Street, San Francisco, California 94103-1741 (publication number USPS 098-830). Periodicals Postage Paid at San Francisco, California, and at additional mailing offices. POSTMASTER: Send address changes to New Directions for Institutional Research, Jossey-Bass, 989 Market Street, San Francisco, California 94103-1741.

SUBSCRIPTIONS cost $85 for individuals and $209 for institutions, agencies, and libraries in the United States. See order form at end of book.

EDITORIAL CORRESPONDENCE should be sent to Robert K. Toutkoushian, Educational Leadership and Policy Studies, Education 4220, 201 N. Rose Ave., Indiana University, Bloomington, IN 47405.

New Directions for Institutional Research is indexed in *CIJE: Current Index to Journals in Education* (ERIC), *Contents Pages in Education* (T&F), and *Current Abstracts* (EBSCO).

Microfilm copies of issues and chapters are available in 16mm and 35mm, as well as microfiche in 105mm, through University Microfilms, Inc., 300 North Zeeb Road, Ann Arbor, Michigan 48106-1346.

www.josseybass.com

THE ASSOCIATION FOR INSTITUTIONAL RESEARCH was created in 1966 to benefit, assist, and advance research leading to improved understanding, planning, and operation of institutions of higher education. Publication policy is set by its Publications Committee.

Contents

EDITOR'S NOTES

As constituency demands for accountability in educational practices have
grown, institutional researchers have become ever more involved in planning to improve institutional efficiency and effectiveness. Stakeholders create the blueprint for the planning process, and personnel from various units
are strategically selected to address a wide array of objectives to reach institutional goals. We, the institutional researchers, have played the role of data
stewards to present vital data and information at each stage of institutional
planning. Increasingly, however, institutional researchers are being asked to
provide information to decision makers in formats that are more useful for
their work and to help guide them in the use of this information. How to
arrange and convert data from different sources into effective tools for decision making is a challenge.

Given the significance of the issues discussed in the planning process,
institutional researchers ensure that no data and information are overlooked.
However, vast amounts of information that are presented in tables are often
overwhelmingly detailed and compel refinement on behalf of stakeholders,
such as retention rates by student type and semester, number of expected
college-bound high school graduates by high school, or student credit hours
produced by faculty type and academic programs, to name a few. It becomes
necessary for institutional researchers to seek creative and systematic ways
to introduce data as an effective aid that will lead to fruitful outcomes of
decision making.

The chapters in this volume of New Directions for Institutional
Research discuss alternative approaches and new directions to existing
issues in the area of institutional planning. Rapid advancement in technologies, particularly in software programs and Web applications, allows us to
process and present data and information we were not able to in even the
recent past. The chapter authors are familiar with such software programs
and Web applications and use them within the scope of their practice. Thus,
this volume showcases innovative techniques developed by the chapter
authors and unique planning experiences revolving around new technologies in the area of institutional research practice.

Chapter One, by Richard A. Voorhees, addresses mixed methods in
institutional planning. Voorhees proposes the integration of quantitative and
qualitative data in strategic planning and provides examples in the area of
competitor analysis and enrollment projection. He also explores external
data sources and their utility in his examples.

NEW DIRECTIONS FOR INSTITUTIONAL RESEARCH, no. 137, Spring 2008 © Wiley Periodicals, Inc.
Published online in Wiley InterScience (www.interscience.wiley.com) • DOI: 10.1002/ir.234

1

In Chapter Two, Patricia J. McClintock and Kevin J. G. Snider present a comprehensive case study of recruitment planning at a research-intensive institution. They discuss a systematic process to develop recruitment strategies using both quantitative and qualitative data. They detail organizational obstacles in changing institutional cultures and map new target areas for recruitment, as well as techniques for tracking potential students. In addition, they include decision-making tools such as real-time interactive programs and Web applications that were used in their recruitment efforts.

In Chapter Three, Christopher J. Maxwell discusses his planning experiences in implementing an institution-wide reporting system at a large research-extensive institution. He describes advantages of the SAS/IntrNet system over other alternatives and addresses the political and technical challenges encountered during the implementation process. Feedback and recommendations are provided for those who may be involved in the planning for new reporting system implementation.

Chapter Four discusses how an application of HTML serves as an effective tool to assist decision makers in using external data. Iryna Y. Johnson illustrates step-by-step an HTML application using Indiana high school data obtained from the Indiana Department of Education. This technique is also incorporated in the recruitment planning in Chapter Two by McClintock and Snider.

In Chapter Five, Douglas K. Anderson, Bridgett J. Milner, and Chris J. Foley discuss techniques to transform data and information into user-oriented formats. After illustrating effective displays in table format, they provide techniques to link admission data to geographical information, followed by simulation models that they developed to project institutional enrollment by ability and admission standards.

Yonghong Jade Xu and I describe an application of Bayesian belief network (BBN) for institutional type classification in Chapter Six. We first discuss methodological advantages of BBN over traditional statistical techniques, followed by an example of BBN analysis. Using the National Study of Postsecondary Faculty (NSOPF: 04) data set, we examine an array of institutional characteristics and their impact on an institution's disposition in Carnegie classification. The chapter, which focuses on the utility of the study results, illustrates an interactive program that allows one to observe how changes in parameter values affect the classification.

Chapter Seven explores a longitudinal approach to student departure modeled to assist in institutional retention efforts. Intervention strategies to reduce student attrition rates are more effective when timing of students at risk of departure is known. I compare studies that evolved around existing retention theories and ones in which dimensions of departure timing are incorporated and present examples of real-time interactive tools to display departure risks of students over time.

In the final chapter, I highlight a few thoughts for each chapter. While each contributing author in this volume has a unique background and role in institutions of higher education, such as administrators, consultants, programmers, researchers, and scholars, we all share one common thread in our practice: data and research findings drive institutional planning. We are also concerned that data and research findings are used in the most effective way. As a result, we search for inventive means to improve the utility of data and information we provide. I hope that these chapters will stimulate readers to seek creative approaches to support institutional planning.

Terry T. Ishitani
Editor

TERRY T. ISHITANI *is an assistant professor in the educational research program at the University of Memphis.*

NEW DIRECTIONS FOR INSTITUTIONAL RESEARCH • DOI: 10.1002/ir

1

This chapter illustrates how the application of mixed methods, combining quantitative and qualitative information, can be used in institutional planning.

Applying Mixed Methods Techniques in Strategic Planning

Richard A. Voorhees

In its most basic form, strategic planning is a process of anticipating change, identifying new opportunities, and executing strategy. Strategic planning can also be described as idea management in which new ideas are developed (or brainstormed), categorized, processed, and implemented. It is a journey that begins best when appropriate data, drawn from many sources and using multiple techniques, are transformed into actionable information. Contrasted to pedestrian information, actionable information makes obvious the next steps an institution should consider. For example, understanding the simple fact that an institution's enrollment is increasing or decreasing is, for the most part, conventional wisdom on most campuses. However, understanding what market segments are growing and the institution's penetration rate of those segments helps the institution understand what actions may be needed to manage growth and should create an appetite for more actionable information.

The use of mixed methods, blending quantitative and qualitative analytical techniques and data, in the process of assembling a strategic plan can help to ensure a successful outcome. The quantitative paradigm helps strategic planners to describe the "what" in an organization, while the qualitative paradigm can answer the "why." Qualitative methods generally provide a better understanding of institutional context, especially as perceptions emerge in the course of individual interviews, focus groups, and strategy sessions, as illustrated here. Quantitative methodologies provide an assessment of how

NEW DIRECTIONS FOR INSTITUTIONAL RESEARCH, no. 137, Spring 2008   © Wiley Periodicals, Inc.
Published online in Wiley InterScience (www.interscience.wiley.com) • DOI: 10.1002/ir.235

the institution is currently functioning (or not functioning). Two quantitative techniques that I have found to be both helpful to strategic planning processes and evocative—developing a competitor analysis and constructing enrollment scenarios—also are illustrated here. (For other mixed techniques used in strategic planning processes, see Voorhees, 2007.)

Arrays of quantitative data are necessary to produce a quality planning document. Planning documents are even further distinguished when they present charts and graphs of data. However, there is no guarantee that such data are the right data to consider in the strategic process unless they have been informed by qualitative techniques. The use of qualitative techniques in isolation, however, seldom provides a balanced or overall picture of an institution's overall functioning. In the examples offered here, production of a quantitatively oriented analysis is animated through purposeful conversations.

Mixed Techniques

A successful model for strategic planning incorporates quantitative and qualitative data collection symbiotically. Tashakkori and Teddlie (2003) suggest three temporal sequences for combining quantitative and qualitative data: (1) concurrently, in which two types of data are collected and analyzed in parallel; (2) sequentially, in which one type of datum provides a basis for collection of another type; and (3) conversion, where the data are "qualitized" or "quantitized" and analyzed again. Strategic planning is a journey; so too is the use of mixed methods.

Necessary Conversations

Strategic planning requires a high level of communication skill on the part of the planning facilitator. In general, wider facilitator engagement with institutional stakeholders leads directly to a more successful process and final product. The conversations that are part of this engagement cannot be casual, however. They need to draw on available quantitative data and require a good deal of preplanning.

Interviewing Key Stakeholders. Skillful interviews can yield helpful qualitative information to the strategic planning process. A necessary first ingredient is for the interviewer to establish rapport with the interviewee. In general, the more that the interviewer prepares for these interviews, the deeper that she or he understands how basic institutional data form an overall picture of the institution, and the better information these interviews will yield. The interviewee will quickly determine whether the interviewer has prepared properly based on the institutional knowledge he or she brings to the interview session. Although quantitative data indicate the extent to which outcomes are being met, qualitative interviews speak more to how the participants feel about how human processes are working within the institution. Understanding where barriers to progress lie and what previous efforts have been ushered forth to deal with those barriers is key to formulating future strategy. Because mobilizing participants is important to the success of future actions, a deep understanding of their perceptions advances the strategic planning agenda.

The results of qualitative interviews themselves may uncover new sources of an institution's quantitative data or may offer new meaning for existing data. To ensure that those conversations yield maximum return, it always is recommended that the preparation for interviews with key stakeholders—a qualitative process—be augmented by analyses of existing institutional data resulting from quantitative processes. Careful structuring of these interviews ensures that actionable data are captured from a wide variety of sources.

Focus Groups. The term *focus group* has taken on multiple meanings as a research technique and is frequently misused. It has been used to describe casual conversations with more than several people in random settings, a clear misuse of the concept (Fern, 2001). More appropriately, a focus group is a deliberate event planned to gather specific information. It has a structure that the facilitator and the participants understand. Well-planned and well-executed focus groups are a qualitative exercise involving a protocol of questions designed to elicit communication while simultaneously not circumscribing meaningful dialogue. In the same way that the interviewer preparation for one-on-one interviews requires intimate knowledge of the institution to be effective, focus group preparation requires the interviewer to understand underlying issues facing the institution's strategic planning process initially and how participant perspectives of those issues can help bring insider information to the table.

Scheduling focus groups in higher education institutions can be difficult, especially if the groups are constituted from within the institution. Finding a time that works for all potential participants is not always possible. Separate focus groups scheduled for students, administrators, and community stakeholders may not only be difficult to organize, they may also produce low attendance. If the goal is for the focus groups to provide an avenue for participants to learn from one another's perspective, selecting only those participants who are alike does little to advance that goal. My experience holds that focus groups can be helpful for strategic planning, but that heterogeneous groups organized to simultaneously represent the total institution produce deeper communication while providing the opportunity to learn about the institution.

Large Group Strategy Sessions. Holding large group meetings designed to promote an interchange of ideas about strategic issues facing an organization is a highly effective strategic planning technique. Strategic planning bodes change for an institution. Properly executed strategy sessions with faculty and staff can lend support for that change. Although these gatherings are sometimes labeled as focus groups, their purpose is somewhat different because they are intended to produce two-way learning. In my experience, few stakeholders have been exposed to the concept of actionable data to make meaningful contributions to strategic planning.

Strategy sessions are a way of educating stakeholders about actionable information and issues that are critical to their institution. Strategy sessions are also a way for the facilitator to learn about what issues stakeholders see as critical and to capture those nuances through deep listening to students, faculty, and administrators and their wide range of perspectives and opinions.

As the name implies, strategy sessions are meant to be high-level discussions. Certainly participants who view themselves as proactive may be more attracted to the strategy session nomenclature than to the more academic-sounding "focus group." Unlike a focus group in which opinions and perspectives are gathered from participants in a one-way fashion, the facilitator of a strategy session seeks to guide a dialogue among the participants about qualitative and quantitative data and what those data may say about the institution's future. Carefully designed so that all participants share a foundation of common quantitative data, strategy sessions in reality become brainstorming sessions in which new ideas can be processed across a range of participants. They typically begin with a presentation of quantitative data about the institution's internal and external trends, followed by a series of questions developed beforehand intended to elicit discussion.

It is common that many participants have strong opinions about an institution's future; common knowledge about the institution's current functioning as expressed in quantitative terms, however, is more elusive. It becomes a key outcome of strategy sessions, then, to acquaint participants with data and explain where those data arise, as well as what they mean to the institution's future. Because the success of an institution's future strategy depends on having credible data, strategy sessions and the process of certifying those data through group processes can play a major role in creating buy-in for an institution's strategic plan.

Competitor Analyses

Institutions may be only partially aware of the profiles of their competitors. Still fewer institutions may have a comprehensive overview of the instructional programs over which much of this competition is driven. As a concept, competitor analysis is well known in the business world (Porter, 1998), but it has had limited currency in higher education. Knowing this key information can be the basis for creating new programs or modifying existing programs that can form a market niche. It can also identify programs that may be redundant within either the geographical space within which the institution competes for students or wider markets in which the institution competes. These data can also be used to look at the entire institutional array of programs to determine whether niches now exist or could be created.

Creating a competitor analysis begins by identifying a list of competitor institutions. Decisions need to be made about whether competitors should be assembled from a fixed geographical region, a list of similar or peer institutions that are more geographically dispersed, or some combination of both. Institutions that lack a predefined list of peer institutions can use the National Center for Education Statistics' (NCES) IPEDS (Integrated Postsecondary Education Data System) Executive Peer Tool or the Peer Analysis System (PAS) to automatically generate a list of comparison institutions. Institutions also may choose to create their own custom list from existing IPEDS variables or calculated variables, subject to certain qualifications. These tools are available on the NCES Web site at http://nces.ed.gov/ipedspas.

Institutions that wish to limit their analyses to a specified geographical area, a technique that logically fits most community colleges, can use another NCES product, the College Navigator (available at http://nces.ed.gov/collegenavigator), to generate a list of comparative institutions. This tool allows institutions to define a list of institutions based on any combination of seven criteria: institution type, institution level, religious affiliation, location, distance from institution, program or major, and award level. Choosing to create a comparison group based on distance from the institution's postal code is often a logical first cut through an institution's potential universe of comparison institutions.

For institutions located in densely populated urban areas where a number of institutions exist, a range of sixty miles is adequate to generate a list of comparison institutions. The sixty-mile threshold would seem to capture the maximum distance a nontraditional student would commute for a unique or niche program. For rural institutions, the range of miles could be set at a higher threshold because competition is likely to be less and programs can assume niche-like qualities simply because of this lack of competition. Aside from distance, institutions need to make other decisions about whether to narrow their competitor group based on other criteria available from COOL. The more criteria that are applied, however, the more the final results exclude institutions from the comparison group, a practice that would seem to defeat the goal of scanning an entire geographical area for competition.

Once there is agreement about the list of competing institutions, identifying competing programs offered by those institutions is much more painstaking. Although the COOL site provides a mechanism to select programs as a variable, those program categories are too broad to be immediately helpful. The Peer Analysis System also permits users to compare "types of educational offerings" (occupational, academic, continuing professional, recreational or avocational, and adult basic remedial or high school equivalent) and allows users to retrieve completions data organized into two-digit Classification of Instructional Program (CIP) categories. The information generated by either PAS data set is too broad to allow institutions to compare their instructional programs. If the goal is to gain some precision in a competitor analysis, there is no substitute for visiting the Web site of each competing institution to gather a list of programs that the institution offers and the exact nomenclature of those programs.

NEW DIRECTIONS FOR INSTITUTIONAL RESEARCH • DOI: 10.1002/ir

Identifying each institution's programs, the titles of those programs, and their content is necessary for making accurate comparisons of institutions. This is at once a science and an art. A program in accounting, for example, might also include options for nonprofit accounting, a fact that would be hidden within a simple two-digit CIP description. A reading of program course descriptions might lead to the conclusion that a given program is slanted toward large nonprofit organizations, while other nonprofit accounting programs may be designed specifically for small, community-based action organizations. Although a six-digit CIP code cannot capture all elements of a program's intent, it can provide a more precise classification than its broader two-digit identifier. The 2000 CIP scheme was broadened over its predecessors to capture a wider variety of career programs, particularly programs that are allied with advances in technology. Subbaccalaureate institutions benefit from the wider variety of CIP codes that allow them to capture, or better capture, their instructional programs. The researcher's task, then, becomes one of examining each institution's programs as stated either on its Web site or in its catalogue and assigning a six-digit CIP code to each program.

On behalf of institutions engaged in strategic planning, I have used Microsoft Excel to collect program titles from competitor institutions using the Web. I then created a spreadsheet with rows assigned for program titles and columns for institution name, six-digit CIP code, and distance from the institution. The astute reader will recognize that there is no column for program enrollment because there usually is no public source for enrollments at the program level. Occasionally institutional fact books report program enrollments, but when these data exist, they are typically reported in broad areas such as the two-digit CIP code classification. An alternative, and not a quick alternative, would be to survey competitor schools to obtain enrollments on a program-by-program basis. Where data-sharing consortia exist, such as the California Partnership for Achieving Student Success (Cal-PASS, www.calpass.org), this task is perhaps surmountable. Individual institutions requesting this type of information from their own comparison list are likely to meet with some frustration because receiving institutions are under no obligation to report these data and in fact may be reluctant to release program-by-program enrollment data.

Assembling a competitor analysis is not a substitute for rigorous analysis of an institution's own programs. A program in title is just a program in title. Internally it is critical that the institution understands where its own program enrollment trends are headed on a quantitative basis. It is important also to understand the history of program evolution within one's own institution, leading to conclusions about why certain programs are given certain titles. A competitor analysis without an understanding of the culture of one's own institution may be a fool's errand. Not all programs found on institutional Web sites reflect current realities, either by design or neglect. My work in assembling competitor analyses for colleges in five states has yielded more than three hundred separate program titles cross-walked to six-digit CIP code. (An example of a program competitor analysis and the subsequently illustrated enrollment scenarios can be downloaded in pdf format from the Broward Community College master plan Web site at www. broward.edu/masterplan.) This list, which is available from me, can provide a jump-start for brainstorming new programs for institutions pursuing new directions in academic programming.

Enrollment Simulations

Enrollment simulations are a second quantitatively oriented technique useful for strategic planning and can engage an institution in considering its future and how its own actions (or lack thereof) will influence that future. Many institutions create enrollment projections based on a variety of techniques (see, for example, Brinkman and McIntyre, 1997). I have a preference for projecting future institutional enrollments from two key pieces of information: (1) current enrollments at the institution and (2) actual and projected population counts for the institution's catchment area. Unduplicated head count data are obtained for the most recently concluded academic year. Population counts and projections are gathered from either the U.S. Census Bureau or, ideally, a state or local agency that predicts disaggregated population growth by race, gender, and age. The more disaggregated the population data are, the more precisely market shares can be established. Second, an increase in precision is also gained when institutions such as community colleges and regional state universities draw students from a narrow geographical or catchment area.

Calculating market shares from external data and summing those shares to account for an institution's current enrollment produces a projection that operates in concert with predicted population growth and shifts within those growth patterns. Because projecting enrollments is an inexact science, the maximum number of years that an enrollment projection can be expected to be accurate is perhaps no more than twenty. Although a baseline projection is fundamental to strategic planning, it is premised on two assumptions: (1) the institution's current enrollment management techniques, including recruitment and retention activities, will not change during the projection period, and (2) the population projections on which the enrollment projections are based are accurate and remain the same during the projection period. The first assumption does not require the institution to do anything new and for this reason is often termed a "status quo" projection.

Use of these segments allows the analyst to model the effect of deliberate institutional decisions on future enrollments. These scenarios are developed to demonstrate the effect of increasing a particular segment by a preselected proportion, most often 2 percent over a five-year period. Other, higher thresholds can be set to match the institution's aspirations and capabilities, but a 2 percentage point growth in market share presents a goal that is likely to be perceived as doable by most institutions. In my recent work in facilitating a strategic plan for Broward Community College, for example,

NEW DIRECTIONS FOR INSTITUTIONAL RESEARCH • DOI: 10.1002/ir

college decision makers were most interested in modeling these scenarios to the year 2010:

Scenario A: Status quo
Scenario B: Increasing the shares of the African American or Black population ages eighteen to twenty-four by 20 percent
Scenario C: Increasing the shares of the total population ages 18 to 24 (the
total college-going cohort) by 20 percent
Scenario D: Increasing the share of the population 25 to 44 (the working-
age cohort) by 7 percent

Based on the predictions for these market segments, these scenarios gave Broward Community College a sense of the probable effect of deliberate enrollment management decisions. Figure 1.1 provides a visual depiction of the cumulative effect of choices through the year 2050.

Conclusion

This chapter has examined a sample of analytical tools and techniques that can be used in strategic planning. These tools and techniques, of course, do not require a formal strategic planning process to have value. In fact, care-ful attention to data harvested through these techniques by the highest lev-els of an institution's management or board structure may trigger the need

Figure 1.1. Enrollment Projections: Effect of Institutional Choices

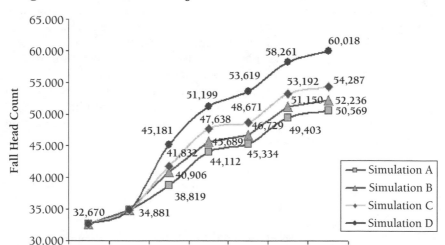

Source: Voorhees Group LLC, Enrollment Projections for Broward Community College, 2005 to 2030.

NEW DIRECTIONS FOR INSTITUTIONAL RESEARCH • DOI: 10.1002/ir

for a comprehensive strategic plan. Certainly there are other analyses that can be as strategically potent as those suggested here, including calculation of instructional program enrollment trends, matches of program outcomes to labor market trends, and understanding one's own institution's instructional productivity. What has been suggested here, especially the use of competitor analysis and enrollment scenario techniques, may be forerunners in a larger quest to create actionable data based on other quantitative analyses that are informed and shaped by the qualitative processes discussed earlier. A judicious combination and balance of both paradigms can greatly improve the practice of strategic planning for institutions that are committed to the process.

References

Brinkman, P., and McIntyre, C. *Methods and Techniques of Enrollment Forecasting.* New Directions for Institutional Research, no. 93. San Francisco: Jossey-Bass, 1997.

Fern, E. *Advanced Focus Group Research.* Thousand Oaks, Calif.: Sage, 2001.

Porter, M. *Competitive Strategy: Techniques for Analyzing Industries and Competitors.* New York: Free Press, 1998.

Tashakkori, A., and Teddlie, C. (eds.). *Handbook of Mixed Methods in Social and Behavioral Research.* Thousand Oaks, Calif.: Sage, 2003.

Voorhees, R. "Mixed Methods in Strategic Planning." In R. Howard (ed.), *Mixed Methods in Institutional Research.* Tallahassee, Fla.: Association for Institutional Research, 2007.

RICHARD A. VOORHEES *is the principal of the Voorhees Group LLC.*

NEW DIRECTIONS FOR INSTITUTIONAL RESEARCH • DOI: 10.1002/ir

2

*This case study illustrates the power that data can have
on successful planning, decision making, cultural change,
and results.*

Driving Decision Making with Data

Patricia J. McClintock, Kevin J. G. Snider

There is almost nothing more frustrating to an institutional researcher than
seeing university leaders ignore data (Bers and Seybert, 1999). The case
study in this chapter examines how an institutional research office was able
to put data to work in enrollment services and produce record-setting numbers of applications, admissions, and confirmations within a nine-month
period. The infusion of data-driven decision making into recruitment efforts
facilitated better planning, more efficient and flexible implementation of
programs, and a greater impact of resources on the recruitment process. An
increased reliance on data has also resulted in greater staff accountability,
improved the division's ability to respond to criticism, and improved overall morale within the unit. Whereas this discussion touches on the tools
used in the university's recruitment efforts, the greatest benefit of our experience may be the impact that data have had in transforming a unit into one
that practices strategic enrollment management.

At first blush, it may be seen as an unusual choice to so deeply involve
an institutional research office in enrollment management; however, many
experts in the field see it as imperative that institutional research be fully
engaged in enrollment management activities (Bontrager, 2004b; Clagett,
1991; Clagett and Kerr, 1992; Huddleston, 2000).

Hossler and Bean's definition (1990) of *enrollment management* is "an
organizational concept and systematic set of activities designed to enable
education institutions to exert more influence over their student enrollments. Organized by strategic planning and supported by institutional
research, enrollment management activities concern student college choice,

NEW DIRECTIONS FOR INSTITUTIONAL RESEARCH, no. 137, Spring 2008   © Wiley Periodicals, Inc.
Published online in Wiley InterScience (www.interscience.wiley.com) • DOI: 10.1002/ir.236

transition to college, attrition and retention, and student outcomes. These processes are studied to guide institutional practices in the areas of new student recruitment and financial aid, student support services, curriculum development and other academic areas that affect enrollments, student persistence, and student outcomes from college" (p. 5). Kroc and Hanson (2003) have an even broader view of enrollment management: "An institutional research and planning function that examines, and seeks to manage, the flow of students to, through, and from college" (p. 79). And Penn (1999) observed that those responsible for strategic enrollment management now extend beyond admissions directors and include many other campus personnel, including individuals who "are institutional researchers or have access to an institutional research department . . ." (p. 57). In this context, the idea of the university's institutional research office stepping in to work with enrollment services, introduce the concept of using data to make strategic decisions, and facilitate the process of increasing market share (and therefore overall enrollment) makes perfect sense.

Background

For decades, Indiana State University (ISU), a research-intensive, four-year public institution, had relatively stable enrollments based on a defined regional area and population, which made recruitment largely a service-based function of facilitating the needs of students who were coming to the university. The recruitment numbers and percentages were not impressive, but there was little pressure placed on the university to improve.

As a result, data used for recruitment consisted of basic reports that provided general information but were not effective in helping to manage a recruitment campaign. One example was a bimonthly report (Figure 2.1) that contained year-to-year comparisons of applicants, admissions, confirmations, and enrollees. The report also displayed these comparisons by college and student type. The information had little value in helping to direct resources during the recruitment season, but there was little need to do so at the time.

In the early 1990s, the situation began to change because the competition in the university's geographical region for its defined population increased considerably. The university responded by increasing its focus and pressure on admissions and began to make enrollment enhancement one of the priorities of the institutional research office. The office was first charged with examining factors affecting retention and projecting the impact of external challenges on enrollment. The conclusions reached from examining external challenges were that enrollments would likely continue to decrease in the future unless the university developed new student niches and positioned itself to be more competitive within them.

The analysis of enrollment management issues requires a wide array of data, both internal and external to the institution, and obtaining the necessary analytical data can be a major obstacle (Kroc and Hanson, 2001). Data

NEW DIRECTIONS FOR INSTITUTIONAL RESEARCH • DOI: 10.1002/ir

Figure 2.1. Typical Undergraduate Admissions Report

UNDERGRADUATE ADMISSIONS REPORT														

	APPLICATIONS			ADMITTED			DENIED			CONFIRMED			ENROLLED		
FRESHMAN	2007	2006	2005	2007	2006	2005	2007	2006	2005	2007	2006	2005	2007	2006	2005
A&S															
A&S/ED															
BUSINESS															
BUS/ED															
EDUCATION															
NURSING															
H&HP															
H&HP/ED															
TECH															
TECH/ED															
SAS/OPEN															
SAS/COND															
TOTAL															
New Definition Breakdown															

	APPLICATIONS			ADMITTED			DENIED			CONFIRMED			ENROLLED		
TRANSFER	2007	2006	2005	2007	2006	2005	2007	2006	2005	2007	2006	2005	2007	2006	2005
A&S															
A&S/ED															
BUSINESS															
BUS/ED															
EDUCATION															
NURSING															
H&HP															
H&HP/ED															
TECH															
TECH/ED															
SAS/OPEN															
SAS/COND															
TOTAL															
New Definition Breakdown															
Grand Total															

showing enrollment trends and comparisons were provided to campus administrators in various formats and portrayed in ways that highlighted the challenges facing the university. Sauter (2005) asserts that one of the most powerful ways to affect change is through information and the way data are presented.

One of the criticisms raised at the time was that the university's traditional local areas would experience population growth in high percentages of graduates, and therefore the institution need not be concerned with enrollments. Presentations using the graphic developed by the institutional research office (shown in Figure 2.2) illustrated two significant points. The first was that the percentage growth in ISU's traditional market was small compared to other universities. University A, for instance, was projected to have a population increase of 19 percent in local markets. The second was that ISU's local market was a low-populated area. University F, for instance, had a negative growth projected in high school graduates over the ten-year period, but the number of potential students in their local market was still three thousand above that projected to graduate in our local area.

New Directions for Institutional Research • DOI: 10.1002/ir

Figure 2.2. Impact of Demographics: Projected High School Graduates, 2007

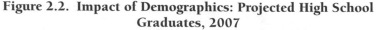

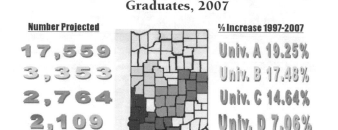

Number Projected

17,559
3,353
2,764
2,109
3,923
5,109

% Increase 1997-2007

Univ. A 19.25%
Univ. B 17.48%
Univ. C 14.64%
Univ. D 7.06%
Univ. E .59%
Univ. F - .55%

From 1994 to 2000, the institutional research office was a pivotal player in the administration's efforts to prepare the university for change and to show how to use data to help identify the future vision for the university. However, there had been little pressure placed on the university to consistently and effectively use data to direct enrollment activities. In 2000, the pressure grew again when the state initiated its Community College Initiative to increase access to higher education. Early projection models estimated that between one-quarter and a third of the university's freshman class would seek this cheaper and, in many ways, more appropriate alternative. Then, in 2001, the Indiana Commission for Higher Education announced the new Regional Campus Agreement. Although this was a positive initiative for Hoosiers in general, its effect on Indiana State University was to further erode its traditional pool of prospective students. Information generated and analyzed by the institutional research office was essential to convincing the president's cabinet of the need to establish a new identity in order to compete in broader and different student markets.

It was more difficult to convince the campus of the need to make improvements in enrollment management. For the most part, the campus was initially skeptical of the administration's argument for a change agenda. Kisling and Riggs (2004) assert that initiating a change agenda requires great discretion and that buy-in across the institution is required. As a result, institutional research played a lead role in guiding a campuswide discussion that employed enrollment and population projections, comparative analyses with other campuses, and surveys to ensure that the conversation remained focused on meaning and implication rather than methodology.

After three years, the campus was working on an agenda to build an image of greater quality on its strengths in experiential learning, community engagement, and selected distinctive programs. This was developed in part to enable the university to attract greater numbers of highly qualified students to the institution. Once these components were established, the

Figure 2.3. Impact of Presentation: Indiana's Changing Landscape

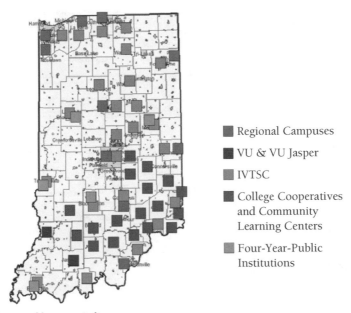

- Regional Campuses
- VU & VU Jasper
- IVTSC
- College Cooperatives and Community Learning Centers
- Four-Year-Public Institutions

Source: Generated by accessIndiana.

office, in conjunction with the president and provost, created benchmarks to help assess progress toward these institutional goals. Figures 2.4 and 2.5 are examples of one benchmark from the Web site.

The institutional research office also developed a host of analytical tools during this period to enhance the distribution of aid, assess student markets, and predict enrollment. In an attempt to directly aid enrollment operations, a research analyst developed an "academic scholarship optimizer" (Figure 2.6) that projected how much scholarship money would be needed to attract various types of students. This model had both planning and logistical applications. Those in charge of funding could identify the impact on yield when institutional aid to target populations was increased, as well as the impact that the redirection of funds would have on other types of students. The model also had a practical application: allowing budget officers and other decision makers to predict how much funding would be needed to increase the likelihood that a given student would come to the university. (For readers who are interested in such interactive programs, Terry Ishitani provides other examples of such interactive tools focusing on student attrition in Chapter Seven of this volume.)

Other attempts to increase enrollments at ISU included the production of transfer retention statistics and studies geared to gain a greater understanding of individuals who transfer. More in-depth analyses by high school

Figure 2.4. Benchmarking Web Site

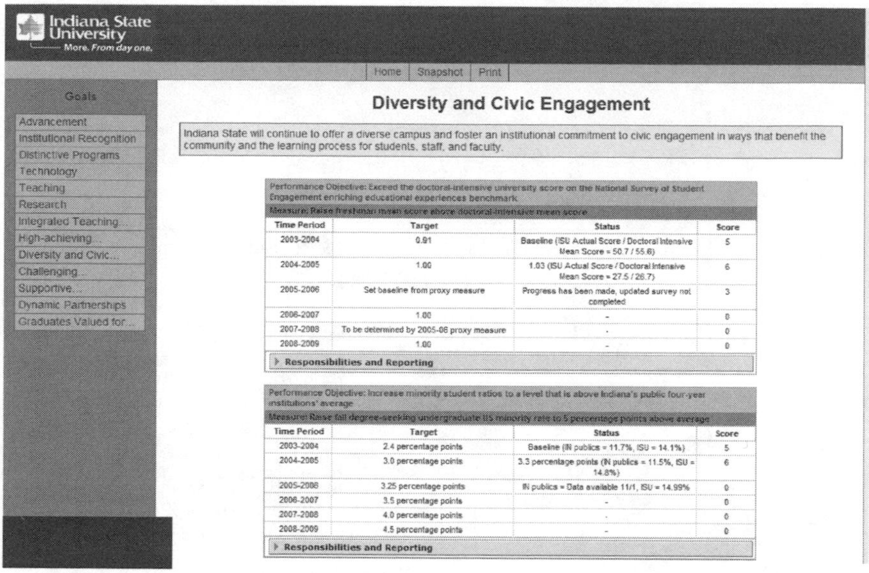

and market share by county were also developed and shared to shed light on these populations. Finally, several meetings were held to offer the services of the institutional research office to enrollment services units.

One of the services offered to enrollment services was to create the high school profile illustrated in Figure 2.7 (for more information on how to create this report, see Chapter Three). Over the past ten years, about 80 percent of new fall freshmen were direct matriculants from Indiana high schools; therefore, knowing as much as possible about these schools would go a long way to gain a better understanding of the students who chose to attend the university and, just as important, those who chose to attend elsewhere.

Figure 2.5. Benchmarking Web Site Specs

Technology Specs

Web application server: ColdFusion 7

Application framework: Fusebox

Database: Microsoft SQL Server 2000

Figure 2.6. Academic Scholarship Optimizer

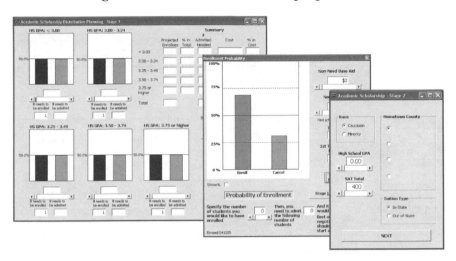

The profile allowed users to look at each Indiana high school and:

- Define the number of graduates who enrolled at the university
- Evaluate market share
- Compare high school performance indicators with students attending the university
- Compare the percentage of students by ethnicity at the school and among the university's matriculants to the high school population
- Compare the percentage of students on free lunch or receiving Pell Grants at the school to the high school population
- Evaluate the success of a particular school's graduates at the university (first semester grade point average, retention, and graduation)

Ten years' worth of data were provided in each profile and produced annually. The project was then taken a step further. Data from the paper version of the profile were combined with data from the Indiana Department of Education and the U.S. Census Bureau and posted to a secure Web site available to university staff using their portal ID (Figure 2.8).

To make it more convenient for counselors who, in some cases, visited rural areas where Internet access was not readily available, the data were transferred to compact discs for them to take on the road while recruiting. This ensured that counselors had the most up-to-date information available during their recruiting trips. The final step was to mail a copy of each school's profile to the high school's principal, along with a letter from the university president. The feedback from principals and high school counselors alike was overwhelmingly positive.

NEW DIRECTIONS FOR INSTITUTIONAL RESEARCH • DOI: 10.1002/ir

Figure 2.7. High School Profiles, November 2006: PDF Version

First Time Freshman from

Fall Cohorts	1997	1998	1999	2000	2001	2002	2003	2004	2005	2006
All first-time freshman	123	129	138	108	106	82	95	99	89	97
Direct Matriculants*	109	110	125	94	87	77	86	82	78	89

*Students matriculating a year or less after graduation

Direct Matriculants from
Colleges at Matriculation

Fall Cohorts	1997	1998	1999	2000	2001	2002	2003	2004	2005	2006
College of Arts & Sciences	24	30	29	36	27	26	34	30	26	28
College of Business	14	18	16	11	6	1	10	15	7	10
College of Education	12	11	20	7	11	12	14	4	9	6
College of Health & Human Performance	4	3	6	1	1	2	0	1	5	3
College of Nursing	10	6	6	2	4	5	3	4	3	5
College of Technology	6	4	5	0	2	0	4	1	5	6
Open/Non-Preference	19	11	21	19	17	27	14	14	9	13
Non-Preference/Conditional Admits	20	27	22	18	19	4	7	13	14	18

Direct Matriculants from
High School Performance

Fall Cohorts	1997	1998	1999	2000	2001	2002	2003	2004	2005	2006
Average High School GPA	2.95	2.85	2.83	2.89	2.79	3.11	3.08	3.06	3.03	3.11
# of SAT Takers	88	89	101	70	75	76	85	81	77	87
Average SAT Math	491	488	479	496	462	492	478	493	466	486
Average SAT Total	978	977	964	999	931	974	966	979	950	963
# of ACT Takers	6	7	8	3	8	2	11	6	2	5
Average ACT Math	19	20	18	19	19	20	22	20	21	19
Average ACT Composite	21	20	18	21	19	19	21	20	19	20
# Academic Honors*	-	-	12	8	12	12	17	8	15	27
# Core 40	-	-	56	49	39	53	57	45	48	54

*Academic Honor recipients also met Core 40 requirements (counts of two groups are mutually exclusive)

Direct Matriculants from
Success

Fall Cohorts	1997	1998	1999	2000	2001	2002	2003	2004	2005	2006
Fall 1 GPA	2.44	2.76	2.63	2.69	2.48	2.84	2.68	2.70	2.51	-
Spring 1 GPA	2.65	2.54	2.59	2.69	2.62	2.80	2.91	2.77	2.40	-
One Year Retention Rate	70%	75%	78%	76%	62%	78%	71%	68%	76%	-
Two Years Retention Rate	61%	74%	66%	60%	53%	70%	62%	60%	-	-
Three Years Retention Rate	50%	65%	60%	52%	48%	65%	56%	-	-	-
Four Years Graduation Rate	23%	18%	13%	15%	11%	25%	-	-	-	-
Five Years Graduation Rate	34%	34%	31%	37%	29%	-	-	-	-	-

Although well received, these and other application tools developed by the institutional research office were not used by enrollment services, and the reasons given provide useful insight. First, because of the pressure being applied, managers were scrambling to simultaneously implement several new initiatives and develop new tools and resources to use in their enrollment efforts. There simply was not enough time to sit down and map out data needs and learn how to use new tools. Second, later interactions revealed that like many outside institutional research, some of the core man-

Figure 2.8. High School Profile, HTML Version

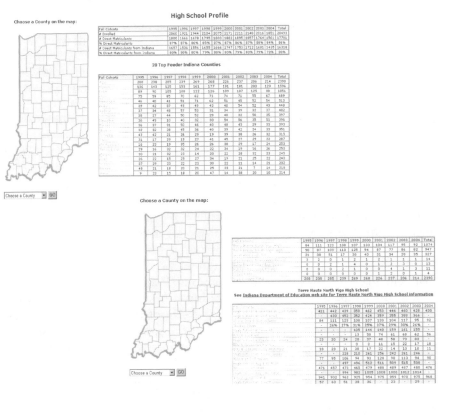

agers lacked an understanding of how powerful data and reporting could be to their efforts (Bontrager, 2004a). Third, as Kisling and Riggs (2004) suggested, the mentality of "that is how we have always done it" was still dominating pockets of the unit; anecdotal evidence was frequently used to justify current activities, chart new courses, or assess problems. Fourth, data were often seen as a threat to the units. If the numbers of students choosing ISU were not materializing, admissions staff members were scrutinized, senior administration began to take a hands-on approach, and the finger-pointing would start. Because the numbers of interested students typically fluctuate during the year, particularly early in the recruitment cycle, there appeared to be a general feeling that one should hide the numbers unless they were good. As a result, the unit was seen as defensive and ineffective when what it was trying to do was create the space needed to manage the recruitment process. Fifth, and what most likely led to the first four issues, was the atmosphere of territoriality and, at times, a bunker mentality. By being perceived as trying to close itself off from the rest of the campus, the unit's organizational structure was not working at maximum efficiency.

NEW DIRECTIONS FOR INSTITUTIONAL RESEARCH • DOI: 10.1002/ir

Black (2004) asserts that the success of enrollment management on a campus may be influenced significantly by the organizational structure in place and cites numerous individuals, such as Kemerer, Baldridge, and Green (1982) and Bontrager (2004b), who have written on this topic. Black (2004) also suggests a shift from rigid organizational structures and the silos they tend to produce, to a more fluid and nimble organization where employee roles and even the structures in which they reside morph to address institutional challenges and opportunities. He goes on to propose that "the enrollment management organization of the future will be more agile and market-responsive" (p. 19).

The first thing that the institutional research office did to work toward changing the existing mind-set and the accompanying attitudes at the university was to make itself as open, helpful, and positive as possible to all members of enrollment services. By showing the staff that the institutional research office was not there to accuse, blame, or take over their responsibilities but rather was trying to bring all units together to work as a team and communicate better and make their jobs easier, the office was eventually able to get stakeholders to focus on working together in new and creative ways that benefited both the units and the campus (Ward, 2005).

By the fall of 2005, the scenario of lower first-year enrollments at the institution was being fully realized. The size of the freshman class had dropped 24 percent from fall 2000, and the cumulative impact of smaller entering classes and declining retention figures contributed to smaller overall enrollment and, coupled with decreases in state funding, increasingly larger budget shortfalls. In late summer 2006, the head of the institutional research office was asked to serve directly in the recruitment process as interim vice president of enrollment services. This request resulted in bringing data-driven decision making fully into the development and management of enrollment services and serves as an example of the power that data can have on successful planning, decision making, cultural change, and results.

Where Are We Going?

Enrollment management is part science and part art. Just as an institution's mission statement shows the way forward, there needs to be a road map that shows where an institution has been, where it is now, and where it is going (Ward, 2005).

The enrollment management goal of ISU was to focus on increasing the market share of graduating high school seniors in those Indiana counties with the largest populations. The rationale for this focus was that the university's lowest market shares were in areas with the highest populations, while the greatest market shares were in areas with the lowest number of graduating seniors. Even small increases in market share in the larger population areas would result in greater numbers of students enrolling at the institution.

For this reason, the president's cabinet determined that additional intervention efforts targeted at specific counties should be implemented in an attempt to increase the university's market share, as well as to test the effectiveness of the additional strategies on the recruiting process. If these measures were found to be effective, then the university could expand the program to include more counties.

The first use of data was to identify areas of opportunity and use this information to convince decision makers of the need to explore new markets. The course for enrollment planning was partly set by the presentation in Figure 2.9. The numbers are rank-ordered, with the left side showing the number of high school students graduating in a given year ranked highest to lowest by county. The right side is the university's market share in counties ranked highest to lowest. The lines clearly demonstrate that the university had its highest market shares in the lowest-populated counties and its lowest market shares in the highest-populated counties.

This graphic was presented to decision makers to gain support for a plan to develop new initiatives to increase enrollments in twelve target counties. These counties were chosen based on their having large numbers of graduating seniors, low market shares for the university, and the feasibility of implementation. During the planning stage, however, it became clear that the university's surrounding counties (its main feeder counties) were also in need of attention. Several initiatives were developed to focus greater attention on issues and activities unique to traditional feeder areas. All other

Figure 2.9. Population Versus Market Share by Indiana County

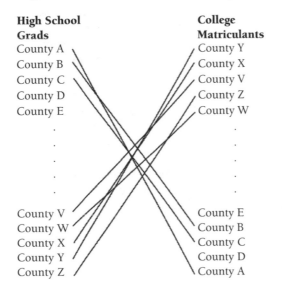

areas of the state would receive the same action, with the exception of a new mailing campaign, that they had received the year before.

One example of a feeder county initiative was School Corporation Day (school corporation is analogous to school districts in other states), which was the result of conversations between the president and provost over the previous year. In an effort to strengthen relationships with the local school corporation, the university had hosted several of the school corporation's regular breakfast meetings and had made presentations at these meetings. The provost initiated this program and had the vision of mirroring much of what was planned with our existing Counselor Day program.

A working group consisting of staff from student academic services, admissions, and financial aid developed an agenda with two tracks: one for high school personnel and a second for elementary and middle school personnel. A special session was available on graduate school and the College of Education to emphasize programs that the university offered specifically for teachers. The provost contacted approximately a hundred principals, teachers, counselors, and administrators in the school corporation. Sixty of the people contacted attended the program, as well as almost fifty university staff and faculty.

The following week, the institutional research office mailed a survey (Figure 2.10) to all attendees. The instrument was designed to determine what types of schools and personnel had participated in the program and how the university was perceived. The surveys were sent out in business reply envelopes to facilitate the completion and return of the surveys to the institutional research office.

Overall the responses were positive, with many stating they were very happy to have been included and hoped that the university would continue to host similar conferences and become further integrated with their schools. Many of the open-ended questions elicited precisely the type of information that the institution hoped to receive: specific and concrete examples that could be addressed and acted on in both the short and long term to improve the university's relationships with local, external constituents.

Data were used to determine where additional effort was needed in each of the targeted counties. At some stages, reports were produced on all Indiana counties, but the activity spurred by the reports were more focused and concretely linked to the following areas:

• *Identifying enrollment targets by recruiting area, county, and high school.* These reports were created for all Indiana high schools and provided to admissions counselors by county and recruiting area. Meetings were held weekly to discuss upcoming activities, current progress, and where additional interventions might be needed. Enrollment targets were initially determined based on assumptions accepted by the cabinet, with final numbers being arrived at with admissions staff familiar with the specific schools.

New Directions for Institutional Research • DOI: 10.1002/ir

Figure 2.10. Perception Survey

Thank you for attending the VCSC activities at on May 2nd
to help us explore ways we can better serve you and your students. Please take a
few moments to complete the following survey and return it in the postage-paid envelope.

Please select your school level

☐ Elementary school   ☐ Middle school   ☐ High school   ☐ Other
_____

Please select your position type

☐ Administrator   ☐ Counselor   ☐ Teacher   ☐ Other
___ Building
___ District
_____

Please answer the following questions. Use the back of the page if needed.

What is your image of ___?
_____
_____
_____

Do your students see ___ the same way? Please explain.
_____
_____
_____

What can we do to help your students be inspired about their future education?
_____
_____
_____

What, in your opinion, is the most important thing ___ needs to do to enroll more
_____
_____
_____

Overall, how would you describe the meeting and breakout sessions? (select all that apply)

☐ Informative
☐ Good discussion and topics
☐ Helped me understand my role better
☐ Helped me understand what ___ can do for my school
☐ I would like to discuss our needs in more detail.
   My name and contact information are:
_____

☐ This meeting was not what I thought it would be

Additional comments
_____
_____
_____
_____
_____

Formulating actual targets for the institution required several steps. First, the target market share for each of the counties was determined. Although a 2.5 percent market share was the initial target for each county, in some counties the university had historically exceeded this goal, so adjustments were made for these areas. Targets for high schools were then calculated and adjusted based on county targets, history of student qualifications, and input from admissions counselors.

NEW DIRECTIONS FOR INSTITUTIONAL RESEARCH • DOI: 10.1002/ir

• *Determining the number of applications needed in October and November to meet enrollment targets.* Once targets for enrolled students were determined, historical conversion rates were used to estimate the number of applications, admissions, and confirmations needed to produce the target figures. The institutional research office also estimated how many applications, admissions, and confirmations would be needed by discrete dates in order to meet enrollment targets. This information provided an early warning system for the institution during the recruiting season. The plan was to use the warning system to stimulate additional intervention activities in the targeted areas to increase numbers at each stage of the recruitment process. The institutional research office was working on the assumption that applications were largely a function of marketing and initial outreach efforts and could be increased for problem areas in October and November.

• *Using data to determine the number of admissions needed by December and January.* Once a student's application was on file, the challenge became how to get that person admitted. From what could be ascertained, the admissions office had vastly improved its efforts to get applications completed and eliminate students who were not serious about coming to the university. The actual pool of admitted students as of June was around twenty-five hundred. This was a critical group for ISU: it was the set of students that would have a high probability of enrolling at the institution.

The numbers of admitted students by high school in December and January were generated and given to counselors and the admissions leadership team. A list was provided to enrollment management that indicated which students were not admitted because their applications were incomplete and those who had not been admitted due to processing anomalies. In either instance, an intervention would be triggered. This would be true of both targeted and nontargeted areas, but targeted areas received additional attention.

These interventions centered on making personal contact with the admitted student. It was at this point that ISU alumni, students, faculty, and others needed to be involved in helping to convince a student that she or he was wanted and would receive personal attention on our campus.

• *Using data to track confirmations and enrolled students beginning in February and lasting through the recruiting season.* Obtaining confirmations of enrollment decisions by applicants was one of the areas where the admissions staff intensified and redoubled their efforts this year; they were extremely successful in getting students to confirm earlier in the recruitment cycle. The plan was to build on this success to further increase the percentage of admissions who confirmed their intention to enroll and then eventually did enroll in the institution. Increasing personal contact with applicants by alumni, students, faculty, and staff was the mantra for the rest of the recruiting season.

• *Using data to assess the effectiveness of intervention strategies.* The decision to focus on a set number of highly populated counties provided ISU with an excellent opportunity to assess the effectiveness of these intervention strategies. The idea was to develop an assessment plan that would allow us to determine which strategies should be expanded to other counties and markets.

The second part of charting the course for the institution was to determine goals and benchmarks using data that would be needed to make decisions while implementing the initiatives. The institutional research office developed several models to determine enrollment goals. One model based enrollment targets on a predetermined percentage increase in the freshman class. The other determined an overall enrollment target based on an assessment of reasonable increases at each high school. In the end, it was determined that an overall increase of 4 percent by county was a reasonable target.

How Do We Get There?

Enrollment targets alone are not sufficient for managing implementation. The use of data in decision making necessitates having meaningful information (in this case, dashboard indicators) that allows managers to redirect resources at key decision-making points. The first task at ISU in this area was to determine the critical decision-making points in the process. The pace at which both applicants and enrollees traditionally presented themselves was examined during the recruitment season. The PowerPoint graphic (Figure 2.11) represents this pattern for past applicants. This pattern

Figure 2.11. Recruitment Time Frame

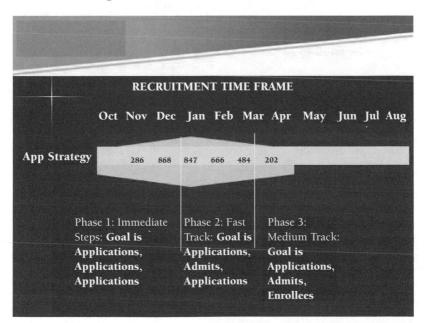

demonstrated that ISU could begin assessing progress in October as applications began to arrive. Changes could also be made January through March, but unless unique opportunities for increasing applications presented themselves after April, the period of solicitation of applications was essentially over. The institutional research office produced a similar schematic for admissions and enrollees and identified similar decision-making points. Reviewing these time lines verified that data needed to be produced that could be used to make decisions on admissions November through June and on confirmations and enrollees slightly later in the process.

The next step was to determine what dashboard indicators would allow decisions to be made and when they should be made. Running the standard report shown at the beginning of this chapter would provide very little useful information for a manager who was trying to determine how and where to increase applications. Because these tactics were largely targeted at the high school level, ISU developed data aggregated by county by high school. Institutional research analysts determined the pace at which to expect applications and enrollees from each high school if desired enrollment targets for that school were to be realized. Figure 2.12 represents the expected numbers for three of the high schools in a targeted county.

The table in Figure 2.12 reiterates two points that have to be remembered if institutional research data are to be used in enrollment management. The first is obvious: the need to create reports that busy managers can easily interpret and find meaningful (Bers and Seybert, 1999). By setting

Figure 2.12. Timing of Applications by County by High School

	Timing of Applications by County by High School							
		2007	2007				Difference between # of first-time freshmen and targeted number
	High School	# of Senior SAT Takers*	Predicted Fall 1st Time Freshmen**	Predicted Market Share	Targeted # of Freshmen***	Targeted Market Share	
County A	High School 1	156	5	2.90%	6	3.62%	1
	High School 2	69	3	4.73%	4	5.91%	1
	High School 3	267	4	1.49%	6	2.23%	2
	County A Total	492	12	2.39%	16	3.19%	4

2004-05 Avg. Enroll/App Ratio	App Needed to Meet the 2007 Target	# of Complete Applications Needed by Date							
		Oct-01	Nov-01	Dec-01	Jan-01	Feb-01	Mar-01	Apr-01	May-01	Jun-01
36.4%	16	2	5	7	11	13	14	15	15	16
33.3%	12	2	4	5	9	10	11	12	12	12
22.6%	26	3	8	11	19	22	24	25	26	26
29.7%	53	7	15	23	39	44	48	50	51	53

benchmarks by high school, the admissions office could determine whether additional resources were needed at specific points in time to meet enrollment goals. It turned out that making the high school the unit of analysis was a crucial component of the success of this project.

The second point is that new indicators need to be checked for congruence with reality (McRoberts, Knight, and Zhang, 2005). As the recruitment season began, the institution found that the completed applications measure was flawed. The numbers of completed applications at some schools were extremely high, while the numbers at other schools were extremely low, and the targets were not working as an accurate gauge. Further examination revealed that applying countywide student application patterns to individual high schools was not a valid assumption. ISU also found that it did not need that amount of sophistication to track progress, so it began to monitor percentage increase or decrease by high school this year compared to the previous year.

Driving the Car

Perhaps the hardest part of this process was getting people to pay attention and use data in their decision-making processes (Bers and Seybert, 1999). It was found that consistency in reliance on data from the top down has been one of the most important ingredients to the institution's success in getting data used. The approach taken was to base almost everything on data, from planning, through implementation and assessment, to fine-tuning each step, and beginning the cycle again.

For example, one initiative was to provide buses to bring students to campus from the twelve target areas in which ISU was not well known. This initiative was based on data indicating that campus visits were a significant determinant of whether a student would eventually enroll at the institution. ISU went one step further and organized caravans to go to a few of the target counties—taking the campus to the student, as it were. Implementing this idea was somewhat of a challenge; it had not been done before, and staff members were skeptical that it would be effective. If previously gathered and analyzed data had not been taken advantage of and acted on during this critical phase, the institution would not have been nearly as successful as it was in recruiting students using this approach.

Another new idea implemented at ISU and aimed mainly at the feeder schools was to create ISTEP Visit Week. The ISTEP (Indiana Statewide Testing for Education Progress-Plus) is Indiana's high school graduation qualifying exam administered annually to all tenth graders. Other high school students typically have several open days during the week for eleventh- and twelfth-grade students when the exam is administered, so the campus took advantage of the open days by hosting several high schools on campus for a program, a campus tour, and lunch in a residential dining hall. However, the critical element was showing admissions staff that data could point the way and paint a clearer picture throughout the recruitment season. The institutional research office shared data widely with those responsible for recruiting in the various areas, as well as with interested parties on campus. Admission counselors and directors met continually during the campaign to review the data by high school. The point was not to lay blame on an individual, but rather to show them that data—good, bad, ugly, or otherwise—were very useful.

Every two weeks, patterns in the data were analyzed to determine where enrollments were higher than the previous year and where efforts needed to be increased. A team approach was emphasized with these data to think through causes, ramifications, and corrective strategies. Money was redirected to advertising or providing buses in areas in which we appeared to be falling behind in expected enrollment numbers. Additional telephone calls and scheduled high-profile visits were made to high school campuses. In this way, institutional research over the course of the semester helped enrollment services develop an understanding that data, both good and bad, were meaningful pieces of information on which action could be taken. More converts to this way of thinking were gained as successes occurred in areas where additional action had been taken as a result of data.

The Back Seat Driver

How many of us have felt like asking a back seat driver to be quiet, only to have a near disaster averted by the person who saw something that we did not? Like driving, using data to guide decision making requires the ability to listen and interpret before making an abrupt turn or lane change. Although ISU relied heavily on the dashboard indicators to determine whether student applications or enrollments were up or down during the recruitment cycle, sometimes the numbers were misleading. For instance, beginning in May, the number of confirmations was used as a way to predict actual fall enrollments. According to that count, the institution had larger than normal numbers of confirmations from the best-prepared students but relatively low numbers of average students. Because there was an incentive to target better-prepared students, the interim vice president of enrollment services scrambled to propose action to increase the numbers of applications of average students (identified as those with grade point averages between 2.50 and 2.99). However, others at the institution began to provide substantive information that demonstrated this trend was an anomaly when looking at that indicator in isolation. Other indicators, such as the number of housing deposits received, were showing that students in this category were committing to the university in sufficient numbers. Checking all of the gauges on the dashboard yielded a fuller picture of enrollment patterns, and ISU was able to stay the course.

NEW DIRECTIONS FOR INSTITUTIONAL RESEARCH • DOI: 10.1002/ir

Are We There Yet?

Ensuring that data would be used in the campus's enrollment management efforts required uniformity in approach. Over the course of the nine months, institutional research personnel not only developed reports that were used in making informed decisions, but also worked to ensure that data gathering became a mind-set in admissions. The institutional research office developed surveys to gain insight into student and community opinions, as well as to assess the success of events. This was meaningful information but would likely be more useful for planning purposes over the course of next year rather than influencing decision making during the current recruitment cycle.

The institutional research office also provided data and guidance to the institution in:

- Work flow design
- Data audit programming
- Assessment and monitoring of the communications campaigns
- Blog and Web application development
- Redesign of application and admission packets, enrollment checklist, and other print materials
- New correspondence for various points of the admissions process
- Temporary reassignment of a full-time position dedicated to programming support for operations
- Management of inquiry and admit campaigns
- Expanding the use of admissions' CRM (customer relationship management) system

As at most other institutions, faculty members are the greatest asset at ISU. Their interaction with students is vital to the recruitment and, later, retention process (Pollock, 2004; Black, 2004). As such, they are asked to contact students at various points in the campaign. In order to make it easier for faculty in the past, the admissions office would distribute paper copies listing the students whom faculty needed to contact. Included was a minimal amount of information about the student, and faculty were asked to return the paper copies to admissions on completion of the campaign. There were many problems with this system. First, because faculty had very little information about the students, they could not make decisions or offer substantive advice while speaking to them on the telephone. Second, the process of returning comments was both time-consuming and inefficient. Missing call sheets, late returns, and inaccurate or missing notes on contacts meant that not only was the institution unable to act on the data being gathered, but the information also could not be used to determine common questions, concerns, or patterns of response from the students.

In response, institutional research developed a prototype that helped alleviate these logistical, efficiency, and timing issues with using data and

**Figure 2.13. Faculty Telecounseling Web Site:
College-Specific Calling Screen**

College of Education

Department	Major	Last Name	First Name	Status
CD & Coun, School, & Ed Psych	Pre-Speech-Language Pathology			Left Message
CD & Coun, School, & Ed Psych	Pre-Speech-Language Pathology			Left Message
CD & Coun, School, & Ed Psych	Pre-Speech-Language Pathology			Call Completed
CD & Coun, School, & Ed Psych	Pre-Speech-Language Pathology			Left Message
CD & Coun, School, & Ed Psych	Pre-Speech-Language Pathology			Call Completed
CD & Coun, School, & Ed Psych	Pre-Speech-Language Pathology			Left Message
CD & Coun, School, & Ed Psych	Pre-Speech-Language Pathology			Blocked Number
CD & Coun, School, & Ed Psych	Pre-Speech-Language Pathology			Left Message
CD & Coun, School, & Ed Psych	Pre-Speech-Language Pathology			Call Completed
CD & Coun, School, & Ed Psych	Pre-Speech-Language Pathology			No Answer

technology. The faculty telecounseling Web site (Figure 2.13) was designed
to help facilitate the spring 2007 admitted students calling campaign. Faculty and university employees logged into the application using the same
user name and password they use to log into the campus portal. They were
then presented with a list of students to contact from their college.

This initial screen not only allowed callers to quickly identify students
who had already been called, but also enabled callers to easily make followup calls to students who had been called but with whom no contact had
been made. Multiple callers were permitted on the system simultaneously,
reducing the amount of time faculty needed to dedicate to the campaign.

Furthermore, faculty members were provided with much more information about the students they were calling. The student's grade point average, admission type, SAT scores, awards, age, and other information were
included to provide the faculty with the information needed so that if students or their parents had questions, they were better prepared to provide
accurate responses and meaningful advice (Figure 2.14).

Finally, faculty members were given a personalized script that was customized for each call. As the caller proceeded through the script, she or he
filled out an online form indicating the outcome of the call, the interest level
of the student in attending the university, if follow-up action needed to be
taken, and other important information. The outcome selected by the caller

Figure 2.14. Faculty Telecounseling Web Site: Student-Specific Screen

Student Information(Click to collapse or expand)			
Name:		Student ID:	
Phone:		Term:	
Major:		Decision Status:	
Email:		Admission Type:	
Address:		GPA:	
City, State, Zip:		Class Rank:	
Gender:	F	SATV - SATM - SATW:	- -
Ethnicity:	White	ACTE - ACTM - ACTC:	
Age:		HS Percentile:	
On Previous List?			

changed the status that was displayed on the student listing screen to one of the following: call completed, left message, no answer, busy, wrong number, disconnected or blocked number. This information allowed staff to quickly and easily see which students needed to be called again based on the color scheme used. This system also gave the institution an accurate and up-to-date list of the status of prospective student contacts. Results were run after each telecounseling session and distributed to admissions staff to ensure timely follow-up and identify common issues being reported that needed to be addressed.

The institutional research office developed several similar Web sites to facilitate both the gathering and use of data. One of these was the Dial-a-Student Web site in which staff made telephone calls to confirm a student's reservation for Sycamore Advantage, the university's new student advising and registration program. This application was similar to the telecounseling application. The focus of the calling campaign was high school and transfer students who had been admitted to the university. A caller who logged into the Web site was presented with a list of colleges within the university. The caller selected a college and was presented with a list of students sorted by department, major, and name. He or she was then able to quickly proceed down the screen contacting students.

When the caller selected a student's name, the program would present the caller with information about the student and a customized calling script. As the caller worked through the script, he or she would complete an online form with information solicited from the student based on information the university already had on the student embedded in the calling script. The customized script made talking to students much easier for the caller than in the past, with the bonus of having a more consistent message regardless of the caller, the student, the parent, or the date and time the call was placed. Everyone who used the system considered it a huge success.

The institutional research office also facilitated the use of blogs for admissions (Figure 2.15) and faculty (Figure 2.16). The setup time and maintenance were minimal, and the ease of use was rated as very good by users. The student blogs (Figure 2.17) were built by the university's webmaster using Microsoft Sharepoint Designer, WordPress MU 1.0, and MySQL. Admissions and faculty blogs were built using the specifications shown in Figure 2.18.

Consistency in approaching issues and finding ways to use data to resolve problems were the most important parts of staying on the road and helping offices at ISU see the value in using data for decision making. Due to the multiplicity of problems, it was frequently tempting to avoid having to design ways to gather data and then use the data, but it was equally important to both train and empower staff to use data to drive their decisions. Using technology and producing applications that were visually appealing and, more important, worked well went a long way toward making this effort a success (Bers and Seybert, 1999).

Figure 2.15. Admissions Blog

Drive, Drive, Drive

Institutional researchers generally have a similar and somewhat unique approach to data. To institutional researchers, data are like a good book or an intriguing picture. For this reason, they are often amazed at how many managers view data as threatening or shy away from wanting to share or use those data. In some ways, this perspective comes because institutional research offices generate data but those data are rarely used to hold the office accountable for output as it is in an office such as admissions. Because of reasons stated earlier, the previous recruitment practices used by the office of admissions were seen as inefficient and defensive, partly based on their approach to

Figure 2.16. Faculty Blogs

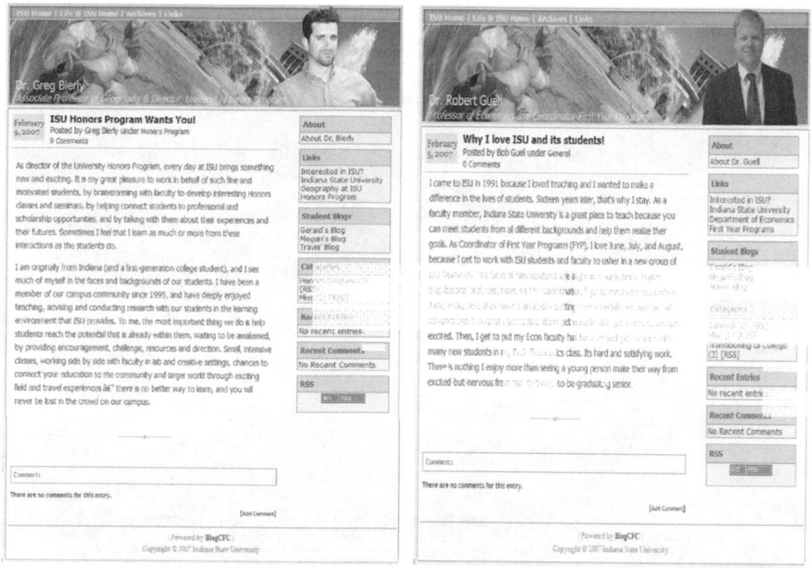

Figure 2.17. Student Blogs

Figure 2.18. Admissions and Faculty Blog Web Site Specs

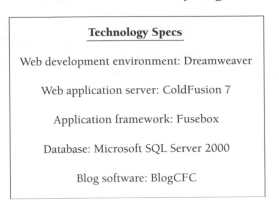

information. They were faced with a catch-22 situation because, on one hand, the campus wanted updates on enrollment, and yet on the other hand, if the update was negative, the office suffered criticism and an overabundance of well-intentioned individuals offering their perspectives or solutions to the problem. The result was that the office eventually tried not to share information unless it was positive, which only served to increase the uncertainty on campus regarding the enrollment situation.

This situation is being conveyed to demonstrate a final point: using data to make decisions can change perceptions of a unit. Prior to the summer of 2006, the campus reacted to the enrollment numbers because of the way the data were represented. It is one thing to share the data, and another to share data that are negative and then to discuss corrective measures being taken based on the shared information. Once the office began to show that it was aware of trends and was responding in ways to change the direction of the information, the campus began to relax. Whether and how many data should be shared depends on the unit, the campus culture, and other considerations. However, those willing to use the information may find that the very process of using data in this way may boost the image of the office.

Destination: Success!

The key to this campaign has been to use data to stimulate a rapid response to its findings. The working team needed to arrive at a decision and then quickly mobilize large groups of employees to do the work. However, the most important aspect of this plan was the need to begin working and planning immediately. The institution was underusing existing tools and was not prepared for the quickly approaching recruiting season.

It was also important that snapshots of the data were taken and analyzed to determine if intervention activities were making a difference. Generally referred to as "closing the loop," assessment means answering questions such as, "Were the goals achieved?" "If not, why not?" "Should special actions be implemented to improve the result?" (Ward, 2005). This would be very important for the 2007–2008 recruiting season in determining whether ISU should replicate any of the processes in a greater number of recruitment areas. It was also important to realize that this was an add-on activity that should not be undertaken at the expense of neglecting historically stronger recruiting markets.

The best way to show that using data to affect decision making really works is to demonstrate success. After using data for decision making in the ways described in this chapter, the new freshman cohort (both in-state and out-of-state students combined) increased by 9 percent, with applications, admissions, and confirmations up 22 percent, 7 percent, and 17 percent, respectively. Figures at the state level (in-state students) were even better: the cohort was up 12 percent, applications up 23 percent, admissions up 13 percent, and confirmations up 19 percent.

Although the overall and state figures improved, of greater interest were the gains made in areas where data were specifically used to make decisions to affect the outcome. Institutional research data were used heavily in the ongoing development of strategies for targeted counties during the campaign, the results of which were the highest increases in all four phases (applications, admissions, confirmations, and enrolled) than in all other geographically combined areas that were tracked. The overall and total increase in applications (22 percent) was exceeded by a 31 percent increase in applications in the targeted areas where additional initiatives were attempted specifically to increase interest in the university. Admissions, confirmations, and enrolled students were also up by double digits (19 percent, 33 percent, and 20 percent, respectively) in the target counties, with confirmations indicating a substantial increase in freshman enrollment.

Because data were used throughout the recruitment process, it is anticipated that significant portions of the increases could be shown to be linked to the new initiatives that were tried this year. The institution will also be able to show what has not worked this year, which is just as important. Clearly the use of data has aided the institution in developing a more robust recruitment effort and furthered the university's promise in its motto to be "More. From Day One."

References

Bers, T., and Seybert, J. *Effective Reporting*. Tallahassee, Fla.: Association for Institutional Research, 1999.

Black, J. "Essentials of Enrollment Management." In M. Rodgers and H. Zimar (eds.), *SEM Anthology*. Washington, D.C.: American Association of Collegiate Registrars, 2004.

Bontrager, B. "Enrollment Management: An Introduction to Concepts and Structures." *College and University Journal,* 2004a, 79(3), 11–16.

Bontrager, B. "Strategic Enrollment Management: Core Strategies and Best Practices." *College and University Journal,* 2004b, 79(4), 9–15.

Clagett, C. (1991). *Institutional Research: The Key to Successful Enrollment Management Students.* Largo, M.D.: Office of Institutional Research and Analysis. (ERIC Document Reproduction Service No. ED332745)

Clagett, C., and Kerr, H. (1992). *An Information Infrastructure for Enrollment Management: Tracking and Understanding Your Students.* (ERIC Document Reproduction Service No. ED351075)

Hossler, D., Bean, J., and Associates. *The Strategic Management of College Enrollments.* San Francisco: Jossey-Bass, 1990.

Huddleston, T. "Enrollment Management." In L. Johnsrud and V. Rosser (eds.), *Understanding the Work and Career Paths of Midlevel Administrators.* New Directions for Higher Education, no. 11. San Francisco: Jossey-Bass, 2000.

Kemerer, F., Baldridge, J., and Green, K. *Strategies for Effective Enrollment Management.* Washington, D.C.: American Association of State Colleges and Universities, 1982.

Kisling, R., and Riggs, R. "Moving Towards a SEM Plan." In M. Rodgers and H. Zimar (eds.), *SEM Anthology.* Washington, D.C.: American Association of Collegiate Registrars, 2004.

Kroc R., and Hanson, G. "Enrollment Management and Student Affairs." In R. Howard (ed.), *Institutional Research: Decision Support in Higher Education.* Tallahassee, Fla.: Association for Institutional Research, 2001.

Kroc R., and Hanson, G. "Enrollment Management." In W. Knight (ed.), *The Primer for Institutional Research.* Tallahassee, Fla.: Association for Institutional Research, 2003.

McRoberts, C., Knight, W., and Zhang, R. "Institutional Research in Support of Enrollment Management." Paper presented at the annual forum of the Association for Institutional Research, San Diego, Calif., May 2005.

Penn, G. *Enrollment Management for the 21st Century: Institutional Goals, Accountability, and Fiscal Responsibility.* ASHE-ERIC Higher Education Report, Vol. 26, No. 7. Washington, D.C.: George Washington University, Graduate School of Education and Human Development, 1999.

Pollock, K. "Undergraduate Student Recruitment." In M. Rodgers and H. Zimar (eds.), *SEM Anthology.* Washington, D.C.: American Association of Collegiate Registrars, 2004.

Sauter, D. "Interview with David H. Kalsbeek." *College and University Journal,* 2005, 80(4), 19–28.

Snider, K., and McClintock, P. "Enrollment Services." Presentation at Enrollment Services Retreat, Terre Haute, Ind., Sept. 2006.

Ward, J. "Enrollment Management: Key Elements for Building and Implementing an Enrollment Plan." *College and University Journal,* 2005, 80(4), 7–12.

PATRICIA J. MCCLINTOCK *is a senior director for planning and strategic initiatives at Indiana State University.*

KEVIN J. G. SNIDER *is a chief of staff and executive assistant to the president for strategic planning, institutional research, and effectiveness at Indiana State University.*

3

The political and technical challenges posed in launching a Web-based reporting system are explored, along with lessons learned over four years of operation.

Building and Operating a Web-Based Reporting System: A Case Study

Christopher J. Maxwell

In late 2002 the Office of Institutional Research (OIR) at Purdue University began to seriously consider building a Web-based reporting system. Purdue had launched its first strategic plan the previous year and was under the leadership of a very data-driven president; unit-level (colleges, schools, administrative areas, departments, majors) data requests and needs had increased as a result. During conceptualization, OIR set two primary goals for the Web-based reporting system: to easily provide for many of the unit-level reporting needs (with the hope of reducing the OIR ad hoc reporting burden) and to provide much-needed standardization of the data extracted (units using the same data definitions and time stamps). The system would be designed so that extracted information could be added to official totals whenever possible, enabling consistency in unit-level reports and strategic plans.

OIR envisioned that the system should only need a user's Web browser to produce any reports, with no plug-ins or applet downloads required. There were several reasons for this. Many Purdue users do not have administrative access to their machines, so such downloads are often blocked. Also, OIR wanted to make the system immediately available to prospective users and to be as intuitive to use as possible, so that no training at all would be required for most users. Finally, it was envisioned that all of the tools deployed initially would be developed in-house in OIR, with a single analyst as the primary developer.

NEW DIRECTIONS FOR INSTITUTIONAL RESEARCH, no. 137, Spring 2008 © Wiley Periodicals, Inc.
Published online in Wiley InterScience (www.interscience.wiley.com) • DOI: 10.1002/ir.237

Next, consideration had to be given to the technology used. At the time, OIR was operating an Active Server Pages (ASP) server from a dated desktop computer, using it to run some limited data collection and survey efforts. It was thought that it would be too labor intensive to design the type of applications OIR was considering with this platform, and there were security issues with the server as well. Other Internet middleware (software that mediates between an applications program and a Web server) options such as PHP or ColdFusion were possibilities, but there was concern with the effort that would be required to make those systems perform the analytical tasks envisioned. Also, the analyst tasked with this project was not experienced in the use of those technologies.

Besides Internet middleware, Business Intelligence (BI) platforms (such as Cognos, Hyperion Intelligence, Business Objects, etc.) were an option that could be considered. The BI platforms would likely have been able to provide most of the functionality desired, with the possibility of drag-and-drop tool building, built-in analytics, data-downloading options, and graphics and charts as built-in features to boot. However, the cost of such systems was prohibitive, and these systems are typically deployed centrally. Purdue University at the time was BI shopping, but had not yet chosen a system, much less had one deployed. Another risk with BI tools is in their licensing, which can limit their access significantly, whereas middleware is open to the world.

Ultimately the decision was made to push for SAS/IntrNet as the technology platform for the project. It is a middleware system, typical in that applications have to be hard-coded and use standard HTML forms as the input to produce reports. The bonus is that all of the analytical capabilities of SAS are available to any Web tools designed with this system. Also, nearly all the programming required to launch a tool is base SAS, besides the design of the opening HTML form. Because the OIR analyst charged with this project was already proficient in SAS, it seemed a logical choice. The cost was on the high end for middleware, in the low thousands of dollars, depending on an institution's current SAS Institute relationship.

The intention was to keep the system to a limited focus, not only at launch but throughout its operation. Purdue had a well-established data warehouse and a very good reporting tool (BrioQuery) deployed system-wide, so the need to build a comprehensive data reporting system (in other words, a Web tool for every available data model) was not envisioned. Also, limiting the scope seemed prudent considering the limited staff OIR was willing to devote to the project. The initial focus was to be on tools that reported on just the most requested and needed types of data—specifically, enrollment data, faculty staff head count and full-time-equivalent data, and degrees. Fortunately, all of these data had official campus numbers already published in Purdue's fact book, the *Data Digest*. This publication had been produced for several years by 2003 and was well regarded and widely used. All the tools initially rolled out would drill into the numbers already known from the *Data Digest,* providing instant authentication to any numbers the Web tools reported.

OIR planned to have one analyst work on the project to perform all the Web tool development, and it was anticipated that this would be that analyst's biggest project over the next twelve months. However, it was expected that the analyst's existing major responsibilities would still be met. It was estimated that a commitment of approximately 0.40 FTE would be needed for the job. OIR was hoping for information technology (IT) support for this project to help purchase, install, and troubleshoot the software as needed and operate and maintain the server. It was thought that this arrangement emphasized the strengths of both areas and would not require much in the way of IT resources beyond the start-up phase.

Technical Details

The SAS/IntrNet software essentially acts as a bridge between base SAS procedures and the Internet. Standard HTML form variables passed to the SAS/IntrNet server are converted to SAS macro variables, an advanced feature of base SAS familiar to many SAS programmers. These variables are then used to control the execution of SAS procedures to generate the results desired as specified by the HTML form. Output delivery system statements (ODS—again base SAS) or DATA put statements then point the output to HTML and the end user's browser. Encoding particular variables as HTML tags enables drill-down capabilities when these variables are displayed in the user's browser. In OIR's Web tools, these would typically be institutions (to include our regional campuses), schools and colleges, departments, or enrollment titles and major names. Alternatively, HTML form elements (drop-downs, checkboxes, and so on) can be produced (using DATA put statements), providing similar functionality. The most critical technical skill needed to work with the system—besides knowledge of base SAS—is the use of SAS macro variables, and the OIR analyst was already familiar with these.

Although not completely sold on the OIR plan for this project, IT agreed to obtain a free trial package of SAS/IntrNet 8.2 and install the software on an extra server as a test platform; this was done in November 2002 (OIR currently runs version 9.1). It quickly became apparent that one of the tasks to fall to OIR was not only Web tool development but any installation settings related to tool development as well. For example, in order to establish the SAS program and data libraries that were needed, the exact code statements and what file they needed to be in had to be provided to IT. This was also the case for identifying any SAS software patches that might need installation from SAS Institute, installing Oracle settings files, and the like. These issues slowed Web tool development at first much more than any bugs in the tools themselves. However, by January 2003, the test environment was working properly, and development could begin in earnest.

Over the next few months, the technology proved to be very reliable, and service shutdowns over more than four years of service occurred only a few times per year and lasted only a matter of hours. In addition, having the full power of SAS for Web tool development enabled the OIR analyst to adopt a can-do attitude to any technical issues that arose during the project; one example is the highly flexible security arrangements discussed below. Also, although each Web tool is a series of base SAS programs individually scripted, they can be used as template material to develop other tools that behave similarly. For example, one would need to take a close look at data set names and format statements to see a difference between the programs controlling the Student Enrollment and Faculty/Staff Headcounts Web tools. If one of those took weeks to develop, the other would take only days.

Implementation Time Line

The first Web tool released was not part of the *Data Digest* series of Web tools that OIR had planned as part of this project. The budget office requested a report, down to the school/business unit and department levels, on staff changes over the previous five years. It seemed a perfect candidate as a test application, because instead of 150 or more pages of paper, the information could be provided to users in drillable format over the Web. Formatting these paper reports is also very time-consuming and can be programmatically awkward, which Web-delivered data tables avoid. Knowing that the budget office expected a standard report format, they were surprised in February 2003 to receive a single hyperlink in an e-mail, but the surprise was a pleasant one because it was very well received. It would also mark the end of an era for the OIR office—the routine production of massive paper reports (up to two hundred pages) with SAS DATA null statements that go down to individual departmental levels on human resource topics such as salaries, head counts, and FTEs.

The next major effort with this technology was political: IT's hesitation in progressing from a free test installation to a production environment. This would require purchase of the SAS/IntrNet software, operation of both test and production servers, and ultimately a minimum two-year commitment. Obtaining approval for that commitment will be discussed, but this was done by August 2003. At that time we released our first production Web tool, designed to replace one of the huge paper reports. Reporting against Association of American Universities Data Exchange (AAUDE) data, it was restricted to a dozen passwords given only to deans and top administrators. Also not part of our *Data Digest* report series, its function was to better organize, control, and deliver the information. (At present, it has been updated four times, although one top administrator still requests a paper report every year.) AAUDE data is something of an exception to the rule that "IR does not own the data," since we are solely responsible at Purdue for its proper dissemination.

NEW DIRECTIONS FOR INSTITUTIONAL RESEARCH • DOI: 10.1002/ir

The next big push was to prepare for the fall 2003 reporting season, where it was planned to release several *Data Digest* related Web tools. The prior tools were either at specific request or with AAUDE data controlled by OIR. Now the office would be dealing with data owners, issues with the data, and data-sharing policies. Despite these issues, Faculty/Staff Headcounts, Faculty/Staff FTE by Funding Source, and Student Enrollment tools were released in October 2003. These were well received, and by January 2004 there was a push to release tools that reported salary data. Under the direction of the provost, a security arrangement for sharing these data was decided on, and a separate portal was constructed for access to the salary data.

With the flexibility, reliability, and success of the technology established, Sponsored Program Services (SPS) at Purdue took advantage of the SAS/IntrNet platform to produce two Web tools of their own (following some training by the OIR analyst), and these were added to the mix in July 2004. They remain the only non-OIR-developed Web tools, and they have been very widely used.

Several other *Data Digest* type tools have been released since November 2003 (Degrees Conferred, Entering Student Test Scores, Retention/Graduation Rates). The SAS/IntrNet service has also been used in data collection efforts relating to strategic plan metrics, some AAUDE initiatives, and other miscellaneous projects.

Data updates, occasional tool edits, and tool upgrades continue. However, the overall scope of the project was reached by fall 2005, and most current efforts are maintenance related, at less than 0.1 FTE of effort by the OIR analyst.

We no longer actively market the project, since our base audience for the tools has been established for some time, and tool logging indicates plenty of use. Initially marketing was provided primarily from demonstrations given at various on-campus meetings (at least ten demos were given from 2003 into 2004). This also provided focus group–like feedback for the project from potential end users. Users were most interested in getting the basic drilled-down data breakdowns desired, showing much less concern about table structures or formatting issues. Graphics were of very little interest, and after including them in the first two tools for the technical "wow" factor, they were abandoned in favor of speed and simplicity. The preferred tool structure was drill-down by hyperlink rather than drop-down box. With the former also programmatically much easier, all tools developed since November 2003 used that structure. The most suggested feature not initially included was an easy download to Excel method, now a feature for all tables in all the OIR Web tools.

It may be helpful at this point for the reader to sample the Web-based reporting system discussed in this chapter. You can fully access some of these tools (Student Enrollment, Degrees Conferred, and Faculty/Staff Headcounts and Faculty/Staff FTE by Funding Source are all public) at http://www.purdue.edu/OIR/resources.htm.

Challenges Faced and Lessons Learned

There were many challenges to address in executing the time line, mostly nontechnical in nature. For this project, they fell into four main categories: dealing with our centralized IT area, working with data owners, handling the data, and applying data access policies.

Information Technology. Information technology was hesitant to support this project for a number of reasons. They were not in general very fond of departmental applications, which in all fairness can be a headache to a centralized IT organization. Such applications might not use technology that fits in with centrally supported platforms, they can tend to be high maintenance (and the central IT help desk will get the calls when they break down), and as a general rule large, centralized IT units like to make the decisions on the technology that an institution employs. Besides these general issues, IT did not see the need for this project since they were in the market for a BI platform and thought we could wait for its deployment. They would have preferred the *Data Digest* drillable reports to be delivered with the new BI system. OIR anticipated that a BI system was likely more than a year down the road, and we did not want to wait that long. (Four years later, the BI system chosen is still not in full production deployment.)

The period of time between the initialization of the free test environment and the deployment of the production environment was the most contentious. A couple of the more colorful incidents included meetings with IT vice presidents in which they refused to even look at the successful test deployments and an instance in which the OIR analyst returned to his office to discover all the SAS/IntrNet compact discs used to run the service dumped in his chair. Ultimately the deal that was struck was that IT would support the project as OIR planned, but OIR would agree to abandon the SAS/IntrNet technology when the BI solution was in place and could replicate most of the SAS/IntrNet Web tools. Since that is still not the case, we remain in production mode more than four years later.

Several important lessons were learned in working with IT on this project. It was critical to the project's success that we did not compromise on the key issues: our pick on the technology, IT as server and software support with OIR as tool developer, and the ability for OIR to act as publisher. Another lesson learned was the value of leveraging the OIR office. Reporting to the president does come with a bit of clout; ultimately this was needed in order to secure the deal mentioned above. An important lesson as well was to always leave conflicts behind and to look forward. Information technology never faltered in its commitment to support the SAS/IntrNet service once the operating agreement was reached, even though some grumblings arise every year when the license renewal is due. The IT technicians assigned to the project always provided excellent and timely service; in fact, there seemed to be something of a disconnect between what the IT administration thought of this project and how the IT technicians treated it.

NEW DIRECTIONS FOR INSTITUTIONAL RESEARCH • DOI: 10.1002/ir

Data Owners. We all know the mantra that "IR does not own the data." However, publishing Web tools can very much make IR look like the data owner. After all, Web tools can provide the information at almost any imaginable level of breakdown, at any time, with the click of a mouse— and with Internet middleware, the default access is public. Not surprisingly, the project encountered initial data owner resistance. There were legitimate concerns about the data owners losing control of this information, as well as concerns regarding the security of the data and policies regarding data access.

We quickly learned some successful strategies in working with data own- ers. First, it was key to involve them early in the process—specifically, to set up meetings in which they were shown the earliest drafts of the Web tools that fell into their data areas. The tools could then be edited to reflect their wishes— whether relating to access policies, details on functioning, or data or informa- tion to be displayed. This very much tended to put them back in the ownership role, and they would feel much better about the process. This strategy was so important that it was occasionally engineered: features would be left out or left incorrect in these early drafts so the data owners could point them out. It was also important to communicate continually to address concerns and sugges- tions promptly. If they requested during a 10:00 A.M. meeting that something about a tool be changed, for example, they could very well be looking at a new version of that tool with the concern addressed by midafternoon.

Finally, although there was some top-down pressure to push these tools out in order for unit-level planners to access consistent data easily in the new data-driven campus environment, data owners were given ultimate control on tool release. They literally had to sign off on the application be- fore it was rolled out. This policy legitimized tools that were released, but it also kept some applications from ever seeing the light of day (an example was a tool on alumni giving).

Data. Drillable Web tools are very demanding of the data: great data for campuswide reporting can look much worse on drill-downs. Some issues we faced were inconsistent or missing unit (school or department) names and schools that split students for official reporting on paper but did not in the database. Other data issues included dealing with official reports gener- ated from dated COBOL programs against mainframe data. By the time these data were warehoused and available to SAS/IntrNet, there was the possibil- ity of small differences that no selection criteria could eliminate.

Finally, even if the data were sound, there were often difficult decisions to make regarding how to report them in a Web tool. For example, which definition of the school level unit (including business units) should we use? There were five to choose from, so which one was "official"? One solution might have been to provide an option in the tool, but that can defeat the "one version of the truth" goal of these Web tools. Should ethnicity report- ing be self-reported or based on the federal standard? We could provide an option for that as well or force the results to use one or the other. Most of these types of questions were resolved in discussion with the data owners, but resolving issues such as these took time.

The time needed to obtain signed-off data (indicating the data were clean enough and the critical decisions on how to report them had been made) from the data owners could easily end up being measured in months. The time required to build a new tool in SAS/IntrNet was typically measured in days. Thus, data availability was a critical limiting factor in this project. One key lesson learned was not to wait until the data are perfect because there are no perfect data. We really wanted the first page retuned to the end user to prominently display exact matches to the official university totals (particularly *Data Digest* totals), and achieved that in most cases but not in all; a couple of the Web tools do not guarantee that. The criteria that usually resulted in data owner sign-off was whether the tool would perform the best possible official data drilling that was available. In those cases, the tools are released with notes and caveats.

Another lesson learned in dealing with data problems was in general not to fix the data with application programming. Not only does this greatly ease application maintenance, but application legitimacy is improved when users can match Web tool results with SQL queries that use the same criteria. The latter point keeps the Web tool from being a black box in which users might not be sure how the results are being derived. In fact, on several occasions, we received requests for the SQL statements that our tools used.

Also, it can be useful for Web tools to expose some data deficiencies (of which they do a really good job). It can spur data owners and IT to make fixes. In the case of this project, it helped in establishing fixes for regional campus school-level unit definitions.

Data Access Policy Issues. This project had to maneuver within both external data sharing policies, primarily with the Family Educational Rights and Privacy Act (FERPA), and policies internal to Purdue—written and unwritten. Our goal with this project was to provide access to anyone with a business need for the information. In general, we pushed a need to restrict as opposed to a need to know philosophy on data access, always suggesting security solutions that were as open as possible. With no particular need to restrict basic faculty and staff counts and FTEs, including detailed demographics, those tools have always been public. Conversely, the AAUDE tool mentioned earlier was tightly restricted in accordance with that group's policies.

The first data policy uncertainty we faced was with the student enrollment tool. Drill-downs can easily expose records on a single individual. The question is: Do you need to protect the fact that there is, for example, one part-time female Hispanic master's student from Colorado studying history in a given term? Is that a FERPA issue? At Purdue, it depends: under the registrar we had when the project was initiated, the data owners considered that a FERPA issue. Our solution was to restrict this tool to on-campus users (a few exceptions were made on a case-by-case basis for external users) and to require a generic user name and password that would work for the other student data Web tools as well. Alternatively, users with current access to the Purdue data warehouse could log in with those user names and passwords, saving them the trouble of asking OIR for the generic access information. Finally, versions of the Student Enrollment and Degrees Conferred tools with demographic options removed were made public. Our philosophy of being as open as possible but still satisfying policy was clearly at work in these solutions. Recently our new registrar directed us to open up the demographic data on enrollment and degrees since he does not consider the above situation a FERPA issue. The previously protected tools were made public, and the nondemographic public tools were deleted; student data on academic preparation of new freshman and retention and graduation rates remain protected due to content relating to academic performance.

The security arrangement for our salary tools actually changed how Purdue had previously shared these data at the school and department levels, where traditionally they would receive salary reports on their unit only (of course, the data are public, but detailed analysis of that data did not have to be). For the OIR salary tools, the provost authorized that everyone given access could see all the data. Two ways to log on were provided: users with current access to the Purdue data warehouse human resource data could log in with those user names and passwords, or individual user names and passwords were provided to those who had a need for the information but had no data warehouse training or access. The latter group was primarily deans, some heads, and other top administrators. The provost did not wish the public to view the opening HTML forms for the salary analysis tools, so logging in is done at a restricted portal, with the salary tool options not appearing until access is approved.

In summary, we released tools available publicly, with generic passwords, with centralized data warehouse passwords, and with OIR-defined individual passwords either as part of the HTML forms or in portal format. In several cases Web tools can be accessed with more than one method. We also limited some of the tools to Purdue systemwide Internet protocol (IP) addresses only. This flexibility was key to meeting our goal of providing access to anyone with a business need for the information, whether internal or external, and yet satisfying data-sharing policies. Particularly gratifying was the project's influence on bending policy toward the more open sharing of information. There were fears expressed by some data owners and administrators that pushing some of these data out with Web tools was going to create trouble, but in over four years of operation, no problems have been reported.

Use Details

As part of the salary portal, the OIR analyst was instructed to track the use of each salary tool in order to keep track of tool use and access. Tool identification, access method and user name, IP address, and date and time information were recorded and stored in an SAS data set. In recognition of

NEW DIRECTIONS FOR INSTITUTIONAL RESEARCH • DOI: 10.1002/ir

the utility of this information in prioritizing tool edits and to provide justification for SAS/IntrNet support by IT, the logging code was added to all the
Web tools. Since February 19, 2004, every primary query to the Web tools
has been recorded (in retrospect, we should have logged since the very beginning of the project). A primary query is defined as a user submitting a
request from the opening HTML Web form. Individual drill-downs, drill-ups,
and navigational changes once inside the tool are not counted. Excluding
applications written for AAUDE, survey research applications, any data collection applications, and any hits recorded by the OIR analyst (most of which
would be development and testing related), 18,644 primary queries made
against Purdue data were recorded from February 19, 2004, to October 3,
2007. This works out to an average of about twenty-five per business day
(rolling over the few queries recorded on weekends and holidays to the adja-
cent work weeks). Since IP addresses were collected, at first glance it should
be quite easy to calculate the total number of users. However, the IP
addresses of some Purdue areas periodically change, and the same user could
have had several IP addresses over several years. From May to November
2005, a feature was added to some Web tools that asked for a user name in
order to help provide IT with potential Cognos users. This was optional for
Purdue systemwide users only, and was not done over a complete yearly
reporting cycle: 124 different names were collected. The total number of different IP addresses collected yearly has trended up: 440 in 2004, 522 in 2005,
650 in 2006, and 599 by October 3, 2007). The 124 sign-ups would be a very
low estimate for the user base and the 600 plus yearly IP addresses would be
an overestimate due to user IP changes. Overall we estimate a current total
user base of around 300, some of whom were using the system but once or
twice a year and others making multiple queries each week.

It is interesting to break the use down by individual Web tools or Web
tool groups, for which we will focus on the time period April 1, 2004, to Sep-
tember 30, 2007, in order to graph the results by completed quarters. See
Figures 3.1 to 3.10 for summarized use information on the various Web tools
used to report Purdue data.

All of the OIR-designed tools (Figures 3.2 to 3.8) are refreshed yearly
to line up with various yearly reports. It was surprising to note the relative
stability of the use of these tools throughout the year; we expected Web tool
use to more strongly reflect official reporting patterns (student reporting in
late summer and early fall, human resource reporting in late fall).

The two Sponsored Program Services (SPS) tools are refreshed monthly,
and the yearly stability of the SPS tool use is not surprising. Overall it was
rewarding to quickly build up and maintain a large user base and to see
plenty of steady off-cycle tool use. The relative lack of dormant times was a
pleasant surprise. One noticeable trend is a reduction in use the last quarter reported (third quarter 2007). A likely explanation is the completion of
Purdue's six-year strategic plan in the summer of 2007 and the resulting
temporary break in the reporting burden.

NEW DIRECTIONS FOR INSTITUTIONAL RESEARCH • DOI: 10.1002/ir

Figure 3.1. All Web Tools

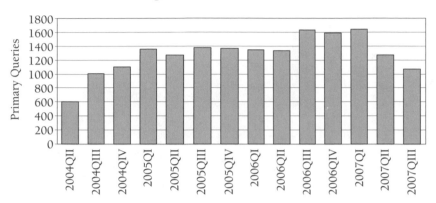

Figure 3.2. Student Enrollment

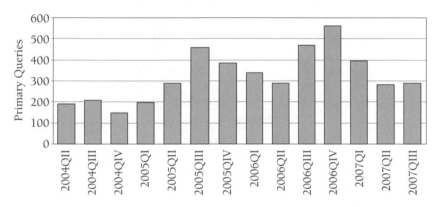

Figure 3.3. Degrees Conferred

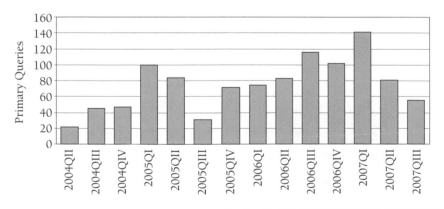

New Directions for Institutional Research • DOI: 10.1002/ir

Figure 3.4. Entering Student Test Scores

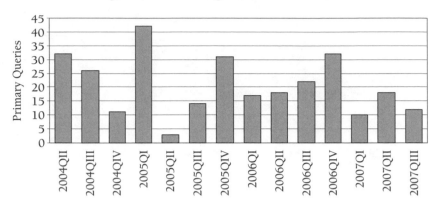

Figure 3.5. Retention/Graduation Rates

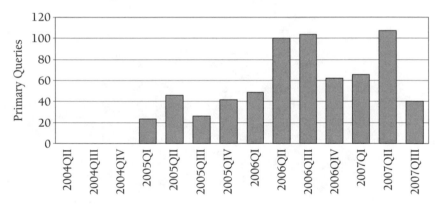

Figure 3.6. Faculty and Staff Full-Time Equivalent, by Funding Source

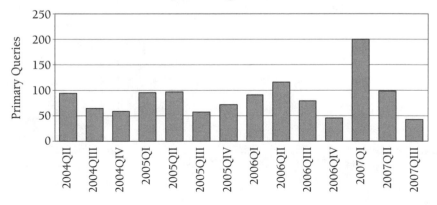

Figure 3.7. Faculty and Staff Headcounts

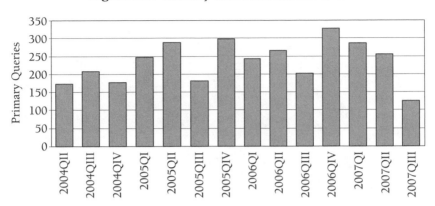

Figure 3.8. Salary Tools

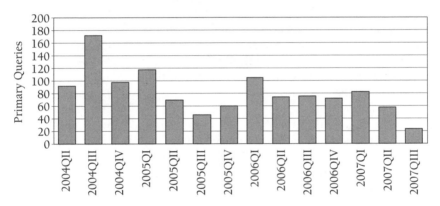

Figure 3.9. Sponsored Programs Proposals/Awards

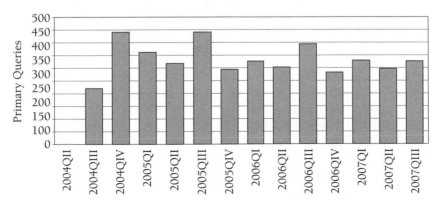

Figure 3.10. Sponsored Programs Expenditures

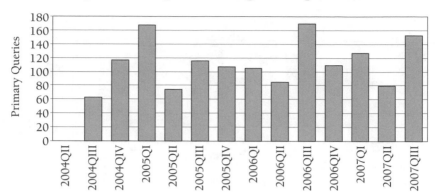

Another interesting trend noted in these statistics is the relatively low amount of traffic (at least compared to basic Enrollment and Faculty/Staff Headcounts) for the Entering Student Test Scores and Retention/Graduation Rates. These data and the SAS table structures are complex, and these tools took the longest to develop technically. This effort was rewarded by the lowest amount of traffic. In general we noted that the more basic the information, the more users we attracted.

The logging file indicates that 9.8 percent of the Web tool traffic is from IP addresses external to the Purdue system (regional campus and technology center users are considered internal). We cannot be sure exactly what all those visits are for, but documented cases (e-mail correspondence) include peer comparison collection, faculty-student research projects, and corporate and marketing research.

Conclusion

This project has been very successful, proceeding on schedule using the anticipated amount of required resources. We consider the size of the user base and the amount of Web tool traffic to be very good considering the limited scope and resources devoted to the project. We seem to have made a very good return on investment. OIR, Enrollment Management, Human Resources, and Sponsored Program Services are all able to direct a significant share of ad hoc requests to these tools. Extractions from these tools have appeared in numerous unit-level data digests, strategic plans, salary analysis studies, diversity reports, brochures and publication materials, and the like. Over this four-year period, the type of ad hoc requests these tools can answer, and questions regarding data standardization ("that is not how many faculty I count in our department") coming into OIR have decreased, indicating our major goals for this project seem to have been met. We have been surprised as well by how much we in OIR use these tools to get at information—after all, we have plenty of SAS programs and Brio queries directed at the same data sources the Web tools use. Sometimes the Web tools are simply faster and easier to use.

These tools are still the source for Purdue data over the Web, four years after launch and counting. Purdue's BI deployment (Cognos) is still incomplete and of very limited access, and the query tools attached to SAP are also in early development. We anticipated about a three-year life cycle for this project and are now well beyond that time frame. In fact, in the near future, we expect these tools to provide much needed reporting stability as Purdue completes its transition to SAP.

We learned a number of lessons that could possibly be of use in other IR Internet middleware projects. The split of responsibility between OIR and IT, with IT providing the infrastructure and OIR in charge of all Web tool development issues, worked very well for us. The arrangement emphasized the strengths of each area. OIR did not have to worry about running servers, thwarting virus attacks, establishing Web directories, dealing with license issues, and the like. IT, with no SAS programmers available for this project, did not have to tackle that learning curve. OIR was given direct publishing rights to the program and data libraries through mapped drives, which meant that edits and updates to both applications and data could be made at any time. OIR leveraged this ability by making timely updates a very high priority. Decisions regarding these tools made at meetings were often implemented in a matter of hours, sometimes minutes. This was invaluable to the customer-driven focus of this project, giving stakeholders' confidence that their issues were considered seriously and would be addressed.

It was also invaluable, especially at initial project rollout, for the Web tools to operate by first displaying the totals reported in the Data Digest (if one chose the West Lafayette campus). The Data Digest was already established as the authoritative source, and that validity was transferred to the Web tools. Users then trusted the drilled-down results.

Another useful aspect of this project was logging tool use. On the surface, these data enabled us to know how much traffic was occurring and where to best focus resources regarding adding data or features. Less obvious, but even more important, is that this information proved the Web tools were used relatively often by a significant user base. This not only provided justification for OIR to continue the project, but put pressure on IT to continue to support it.

Finally, technical issues were not the most challenging aspects of this project. Technical issues tended to be self-contained and always seemed to be either solvable outright or able to be worked around somehow. They only required review of SAS user group (SUGI) papers, Web searches, help files, SAS manuals, and so forth. Specific instructions could be provided to the IT SAS/IntrNet operator if something needed doing on that end. There were at most two people involved, and nobody needed to negotiate. Although we were very satisfied with our choice of SAS/IntrNet, there are many other IR reporting systems using other middleware. That particular technology was simply a good choice for us.

The most challenging aspects of this project were in dealing with data, people, and politics. In fact, politics is an integral part of a project such as this one. Tackling these issues needs to be done with the same enthusiasm that goes into designing the Web tools themselves. Navigating these non-technical issues with any success is very rewarding.

We have received a lot of positive feedback over the years on this project, but a comment we received in our first year is still a favorite: "This is exactly what I need. Now I can sleep peacefully over the weekend."

CHRISTOPHER J. MAXWELL *is a research and planning analyst in the office of institutional research at Purdue University.*

NEW DIRECTIONS FOR INSTITUTIONAL RESEARCH • DOI: 10.1002/ir

4

Because high school graduates are many colleges' primary target population, information on high school students' performance and sociodemographic characteristics becomes important for the recruitment process.

High School Profiles: Application of HTML for Recruitment Decision Making

Iryna Y. Johnson

> I spent the day visiting two public schools in a large urban area in the Midwest. At both schools, I did not meet a counselor. . . . As quietly as I was received I was dismissed. . . . I wished someone would have given me an orientation to the schools. . . . I wondered, "Are none of the 3,000 students in these buildings interested in my school's type?" Many other questions ran through my mind, such as, ". . . Should I come back next year?"
>
> Journal entry of an admission counselor (cited in Lautz, Hawkins, and Pérez, 2005)

The efficient recruitment of students presumes having accurate and current information on high schools before school visits. It is not worthwhile for the institution to spend thousands of dollars on transportation, hotel, food, and mailings if graduates of a targeted high school never enroll in their institution. In addition to achieving a sufficient number of students to be recruited, universities face other goals that involve recruiting students with higher academic abilities (quality) and students who have been traditionally underrepresented in higher education (for example, ethnic minorities and students from low-income families). Information on the academic and sociodemographic characteristics of high schools' populations is important for institutions to use to help achieve these goals.

NEW DIRECTIONS FOR INSTITUTIONAL RESEARCH, no. 137, Spring 2008 © Wiley Periodicals, Inc.
Published online in Wiley InterScience (www.interscience.wiley.com) • DOI: 10.1002/ir.238

Some of the questions that can be posited by admission counselors and enrollment managers in relation to high schools are:

• What are the current primary recruitment areas and schools?
• What are the target population trends by counties and high schools?
• Does the institution typically attract the best students from a particular school?
• Where do the best students come from?
• What are the success rates for students from a particular school?
• What are the institution's market shares in the most populated areas?
• Where can the institution attract a diverse population from?

Answering these questions in relation to a particular school is a challenging task. Each college typically attracts students from numerous schools. Providing trends, high school characteristics, and high school graduates' success for each school in a manner that is easy to access and use requires a creative approach in data presentation.

This chapter introduces an HTML application (referred to here as the High School Profile) that arranges high school information and makes the information easier for recruiters to use. The chapter begins with an overview of the High School Profile. It then shows the information presented for Indiana counties and schools overall and in relation to a study institution, points out the sources of data used, and covers certain technical aspects with how the application was created.

High School Profile: An Overview

Postsecondary institutions rarely have detailed information on the academic and sociodemographic characteristics of high school populations. Therefore, seeking information from external sources becomes necessary to develop the High School Profile. The application used here links the external data on high schools' performance and populations from Indiana Department of Education (IDOE) to the internal (institutional) data. The institutional data were restricted to include only students who graduated from in-state high schools and planned to matriculate within one year after graduating, in other words, direct matriculants. At the institution considered here, direct matriculants from Indiana high schools constitute roughly 80 percent of new fall freshmen.

The profile presents the information by counties. The original Web page (see Figure 4.1) contains an Indiana map and form linking counties to more information about high school students coming from these counties. Information about a particular county can be obtained by clicking on the county of interest on the map or choosing its name from the form. This Web page also presents information on the number of direct matriculants from Indiana high schools overall and from twenty top feeder counties for ten consecutive years.

NEW DIRECTIONS FOR INSTITUTIONAL RESEARCH • DOI: 10.1002/ir

Figure 4.1. High School Profile: An Original Web Page

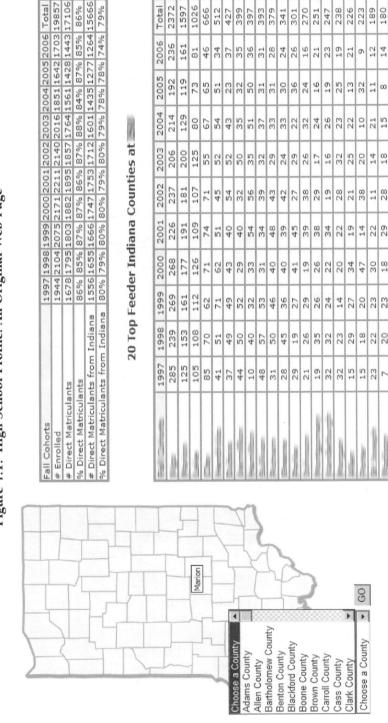

Figure 4.2. High School Profile: Overall County Information and Link to the U.S. Census Bureau

▬▬ county

Of 2372 direct matriculants from ▬▬ county, 1067 came from ▬▬ ▬▬ High, 937 - from ▬▬ ▬▬ High, 323 - from ▬▬ High School, 19 - from ▬▬ ▬▬ School, 12 - from ▬▬ ▬▬ Center, 10 - from ▬▬ ▬▬ School, and 4 - from ▬▬ Inc.

See Indiana QuickFacts from the US Census Bureau for ▬▬ county information

Fall Cohorts	1997	1998	1999	2000	2001	2002	2003	2004	2005	2006	Total
High	123	108	107	133	104	117	95	92	85	103	1067
High	109	110	125	94	87	77	86	82	78	89	937
School	51	17	30	40	31	34	20	35	25	40	323
School	2	1	4	0	1	2	3	0	4	2	19
Center	0	2	1	0	0	4	1	3	0	1	12
School	0	1	2	1	2	1	1	1	0	1	10
Inc	0	0	0	0	1	2	0	1	0	0	4
Total	285	239	269	268	226	237	206	214	192	236	2372

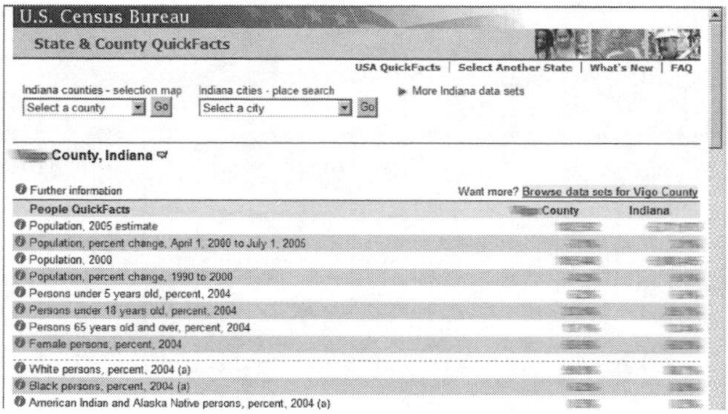

The information by counties includes the number of direct matriculants coming from this county's schools and a link to the U.S. Census Bureau County Quick Facts showing characteristics of the population residing in this county (see Figure 4.2).

A county's page contains tables for each high school sending students to the institution (see Figure 4.3) covering the following data for ten consecutive years:

- The number of students enrolled in the twelfth grade, the number of graduates, and the number of students matriculating to a study institution within one year of graduation
- The percentage of matriculants to the study institution among high school graduates (market share)
- The average SAT and ACT scores of students, the number of students with Core 40 diplomas (that is, required high school curriculum for graduation in Indiana), the number of academic honors diplomas awarded to

students for a high school and for direct matriculants to the study institution from this high school
- The representation of several ethnicity groups at a high school and among matriculants from this high school
- The percentage of students receiving free lunches at a high school and the percentage of Pell Grant recipients at the study institution
- The fall semester grade point average (GPA); retention rates for one, two, and three years; and graduation rates for four and five years.

Preceding the table with statistics on a high school is a link to the school snapshot at the Indiana Department of Education Web site (see Figure 4.3).

Figure 4.3. High School Profile: A School Table and Link to the Indiana Department of Education

See Indiana Department of Education web site for High School / High School information

Fall Cohorts	1997	1998	1999	2000	2001	2002	2003	2004	2005	2006
High School # Enrolled in 12th Grade	439	358	462	453	446	460	428	430	462	459
High School # Graduated	401	339	420	359	355	388	366	389	385	-
# Direct Matriculants	123	108	107	133	104	117	95	92	85	103
Market Share	31%	32%	25%	37%	29%	30%	26%	24%	22%	-
High School # Core 40	-	105	144	140	159	161	155	151	158	-
# Core 40	0	13	58	74	61	68	62	56	56	72
High School # Academic Honors	24	20	37	48	58	73	83	98	98	-
# Academic Honors	0	0	3	11	15	22	17	18	14	24
# Conditionally Admitted	21	30	17	22	14	10	10	11	12	17
High School # of SAT takers	228	210	261	256	242	261	246	253	240	-
# of SAT takers	106	94	93	120	98	113	94	90	85	102
High School Avg SAT Math	497	496	512	511	509	515	508	501	517	-
Avg SAT Math	473	465	479	488	489	487	480	476	495	483
High School Avg SAT Total	994	982	1005	1008	1000	1012	1014	1004	1034	-
Avg SAT Total	962	925	954	975	959	970	975	968	998	959
High School # of ACT takers	51	28	36	37	23	20	29	27	-	-
# of ACT takers	16	7	9	8	3	1	2	2	2	2
High School Avg ACTM	20	20	22	23	24	23	23.7	22.6	-	-
Avg ACTM	22	19	20	21	20	22	22	18	20	18
High School Avg ACT Composite	21	20	22	23	24	23	24.3	22.6	-	-
Avg ACT Composite	22	21	19	21	21	23	23	20	18	19
Avg High School GPA	2.84	2.81	2.92	2.94	2.94	3.01	2.95	3.00	3.03	3.03
High School % African American	7%	6%	7%	7%	8%	7%	7%	7%	7%	6%
% African American	3%	3%	3%	5%	3%	4%	3%	8%	8%	4%
High School % Caucasian	91%	91%	90%	91%	90%	90%	90%	88%	89%	89%
% Caucasian	93%	95%	93%	92%	92%	94%	92%	88%	82%	91%
High School % Hispanic	1%	1%	1%	1%	0%	1%	1%	1%	1%	1%
% Hispanic	0%	0%	0%	0%	0%	0%	0%	0%	0%	1%
High School % Free Lunch	18%	15%	17%	15%	15%	19%	21%	23%	23%	27%
% Pell	13%	31%	28%	21%	26%	31%	31%	36%	26%	34%
Fall 1 GPA	2.56	2.62	2.76	2.77	2.50	2.73	2.70	2.75	2.57	-
Fall2 # Enrolled	90	85	85	101	70	89	69	67	61	-
Fall3 # Enrolled	76	68	68	96	61	80	53	60	-	-
Fall4 # Enrolled	68	63	59	76	49	71	46	-	-	-
Fall5 # Graduated	25	22	22	31	18	24	-	-	-	-
Fall6 # Graduated	48	39	37	51	31	-	-	-	-	-

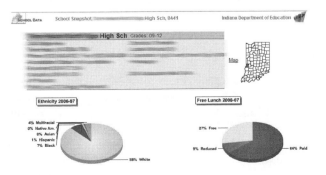

In summary, the information on each high school allows one to evaluate the overall odds of this school's graduates coming to a particular institution, the likelihood of getting matriculants with certain demographic and academic characteristics from this high school, and the likelihood of these high school students' success at the institution.

Data Sources

The High School Profile relies on both internal and external data sources. The internal (institutional) source is the retention database, which contains information on entering first-time freshmen, their ethnicity, precollege academic characteristics and college GPA, indicators of receiving financial aid (Pell Grant in particular), as well as their retention and graduation. The primary external information comes from the Indiana Department of Education, which furnishes enrollment statistics, the numbers of graduates, and the average test scores and sociodemographic composition of enrollees at Indiana public high schools.

The external data have been retrieved from the Indiana Department of Education Web site (http://www.doe.state.in.us/). Figure 4.4 shows the links to follow to retrieve the data.

The following school building–level tables selected from the Indiana Department of Education were:

- General School Variables
- Graduates, Graduation Rates, Dropouts
- Enrollment by Grade (includes data on representation of different ethnicity groups at a high school)
- SAT Scores
- ACT Scores
- Free Lunch Counts by School

To find institutional school numbers for school numbers of Indiana Department of Education, the data sets were originally merged by location postal codes. Federal Interagency Committee on Education codes were available for institutional data but not available for Indiana Department of Education data.

Technical Aspects

The High School Profile was created using the hand-coded HTML, or a simple Notepad editor. Using FRAMES, two HTML documents were displayed in the same browser window. One frame ("Map") was used to display a map and the form and another ("Main") to display the information on the number of direct matriculants from Indiana high schools overall and from twenty top feeder counties (see Figure 4.1; for data on a particular county

**Figure 4.4. Data Sources: Links to Retrieve Data from the Indiana
Department of Education Web Site**

and its high schools, see Figures 4.2 and 4.3). The HTML code creating the
frame set was as follows:

```
<FRAMESET COLS="32%,*" border="0">
<FRAME NAME="Map" SRC="map.html" TITLE="Map">
<FRAME NAME="Main" SRC="main.html" TITLE="Main">
</FRAMESET>
```

The FRAME "Map" (see Figure 4.5) was created to link the school information to a particular county on the Indiana map and to the county's
name on the form.

To link the school information to a particular county, the High School
Profile contains an HTML image map, which is a list of coordinates on a
specific image created in order to hyperlink areas of the image to various
destinations (http://www.htmlcodetutorial.com/images/images_famsupp_
220.html and http://www.w3schools.com/html/html_images.asp). Thus, a
map of Indiana has each county hyperlinked to further information about
high school students originating from that county. The following HTML

Figure 4.5. Technical Aspects: FRAME "Map"

code creates an area on the image from file "Indiana map.gif" hyperlinked to the file "vigo.html":

```
<img src="indiana map.gif" usemap="#indianamap" border="0">
<map name="indianamap">
<area shape="polygon" coords="55,241,83,241,83,249,
81,277,50,277"
alt="Vigo" href="vigo.html" target="Main">
. . .
</map>
```

The SRC attribute in <img> assigns the image to the source file. The USEMAP attribute in <img> refers to the id or name attribute in <map>. The attribute BORDER="0" is used to avoid putting a frame around the image, and the attribute HREF="vigo.html" denotes the file that should be loaded when the user chooses a particular area. The TARGET attribute indicates which frame in a set of frames to send the 'vigo.html' to, SHAPE defines the shape of the area, and COORDS defines the specific coordinates of the area.

Any picture editor can be used to identify the coordinates on a particular image. For example, as shown on Figure 4.6, a user who points at a particular position of an image in MS Paint would see its coordinates in the bottom right corner.

Figure 4.6. Technical Aspects: Identifying Coordinates on an Image

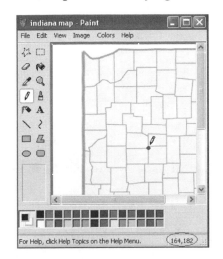

The type of coordinates depends on the shape. There are three possible shapes in HTML image maps: rectangle (<SHAPE="RECT">), circle (<SHAPE="CIRCLE">), and polygon (<SHAPE="POLYGON">).

For a rectangle shape (see Figure 4.7), one should use two coordinates: the upper left corner of the rectangle and the lower right corner of the rectangle:

<area shape="rect" coords="55,241,81,277" href="vigo.html" target="Main">

For a circular shape (see Figure 4.8), one should use three numbers: the first two numbers define the center point of the circle, and the third number is the radius of the circle:

Figure 4.7. Technical Aspects: Shape Coordinates

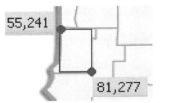

Figure 4.8. Technical Aspects: Circle Shape Coordinates

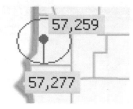

Figure 4.9. Technical Aspects: Polygon Shape Coordinates

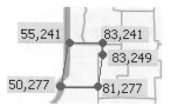

Figure 4.10. Technical Aspects: Alternate Text (ALT) Attribute

<area shape="cirle" coords="57,259,18" href="vigo.html" target="Main">

A polygon (see Figure 4.9) is defined by three or more pairs of *x/y* coordinates. The lines connecting those coordinates create an area:

<area shape="55,241,83,241,83,249, 81,277,50,277" href="vigo.html" target="Main">

The ALT ("alternate text") attribute (see Figure 4.10) tells the user what he or she would link to by clicking on a particular area. For example, alt="Vigo" indicates that the area on the map represents Vigo County and hyperlinks to the information on Vigo county's high schools:

```
<area shape="polygon" coords="55,241,83,241,83,249,
81,277,50,277" alt="Vigo" href="vigo.html" target="Main">
```

The following HTML script creates a form (see Figure 4.11) that has each county's name hyperlinked to further information about high school students coming from that county:

```
<form name="jump">
<select name="menu">
<option value="Main.html">Choose a County</option>
<option value="Adams.html">Adams County</option>
. . .
</select>
<input type="button" value="GO"
onClick="parent.Main.location=document.jump.menu.options[docu-
ment.jump.menu.selectedIndex].value;" value="GO">
</form>
```

Script <form name=> defines a unique name for the form. The <select> element creates a drop-down list. Script <select name=> assigns the name to the drop-down list. HTML script *<select><option value ="Adams.html">* *Adams County </option>* assigns the option on the form to a particular file and creates the following output   (http://www.w3schools.com/ html/html_forms.asp). HTML script <input type="button" value="GO"> creates the GO button. <ONCLICK> indicates the script command to run when the user clicks on the GO button. <PARENT> indicates where the output would be located within the frameset (in this example, MAIN). <ONCLICK> is set to location, where "location" is where the browser should go once the button is clicked. The location here is set to =document.

Figure 4.11. Technical Aspects: Example of a Form

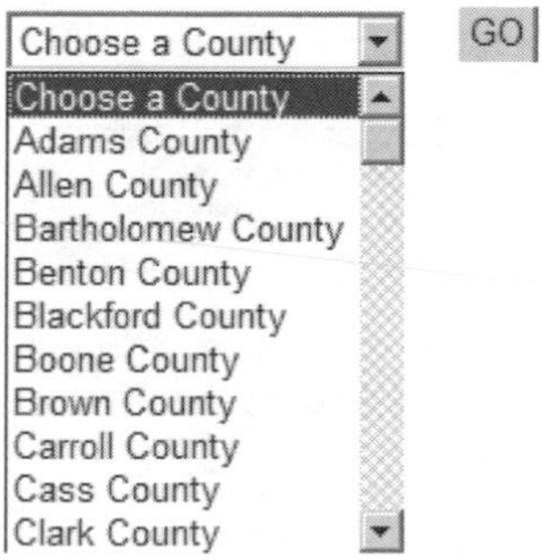

jump.menu.options[document.jump.menu.selectedindex].value.DOCU-
MENT is the current page that is displayed in the browser, JUMP is a reference to the <form name="jump">, MENU refers to <select name="menu">.

Thus, document.jump.menu.options[documents.jump.menu.selected-
index].value is telling the browser to get the value (for example,
"Adams.html") of the option that is currently selected (such as Adams
County) by the user.

The "Main" part of the FRAMESET in High School Profile was created
using HTML tables created in Excel. The data set at 'data' spreadsheet (see
Figure 4.12) was linked to a resulting HTML table at 'Internet' spreadsheet
that was ready to copy and be copied in the HTML file.

Creating tables with HTML is the major technical limitation of the High
School Profile. A more appropriate script would be, for example, an Active
Server Pages (ASP) script that allows linking to a database located on a server
and makes the application more dynamic.

Overall, the current presentation of the High School Profile can serve
as an illustration of the way to present information from numerous schools
in a compact and easy-to-use way. While being covered, its technical aspects
have limitations that can be overcome by using a different script.

Implications

At the planning level, the High School Profile described here assists in eval-
uating the current (and selecting potential) markets for new freshman
recruitment and in making decisions on where and how to deploy an insti-

Figure 4.12. Technical Aspect: Creating HTML Tables

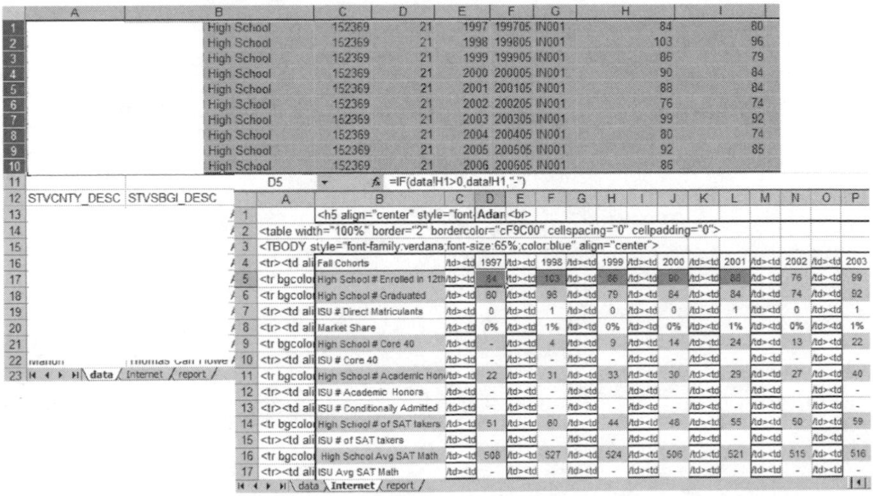

tution's resources to achieve its recruitment goals and strategies. To provide the information on high schools overall and as it pertains to the institution, High School Profile links the institutional data with the state data on high schools' performance and populations (in other words, the high school share of standardized test takers, average standardized test scores, high school locale, and the percentage of students receiving a free lunch). Using past data on high school recruitment and retention allows one to locate areas and high schools that are most likely to produce the targeted number of enrollees with certain attributes (with respect to quality and diversity, for example). Schools that have historically yielded higher numbers of enrollees are more likely to yield more enrollees in the future. Thus, High School Profile allows the university to focus on schools with higher yield rates and thus deploy its resources in a more efficient way.

At the implementation level, the High School Profile assists the university in making decisions on where and how to deploy its resources to achieve its recruitment goals and strategies. The High School Profile also provides valuable information for admission counselors. For example, it can serve as a conversation starter during high school visits and to inform high school counselors of their students' success at the institution. Last but not least, some high schools request the information on their students' success, and High School Profile can save time and provide such a report in a timely manner.

References

How to Make an Image Map, retrieved January 15, 2007, from http://www.htmlcodetutorial.com/images/images_famsupp_220.html.

HTML Forms and Input, retrieved January 15, 2007, from http://www.w3schools.com/html/html_forms.asp.

HTML Images, retrieved January 15, 2007, from http://www.w3schools.com/html/html_images.asp.

Indiana Department of Education. *K-12 school data.* Retrieved January 15, 2007, at http://mustang.doe.state.in.us/SAS/sas1.cfm.

Lautz, J., Hawkins, D., and Pérez, A. "The High School Visit: Providing College Counseling and Building Crucial K-16 Links Among Students, Counselors and Admission Officers." *Journal of College Admission,* Summer 2005, *188,* 6–15.

IRYNA Y. JOHNSON is a research analyst in the office of university planning, institutional research, and accountability at Indiana University, Bloomington.

Enrollment management data must be transformed into information that is accessible, timely, and meaningful. Creative approaches are suggested to overcome the challenges of oversimplification and of reports too complex to be useful.

From Complex Data to Actionable Information: Institutional Research Supporting Enrollment Management

Douglas K. Anderson, Bridgett J. Milner, Chris J. Foley

Producing analyses that are accurate, timely, and simple is a constant challenge for institutional researchers. The stakes are high: when the analysis is incomplete, arrives too late, does not adequately address the question, or is simply too much to comprehend, decision makers fall back on anecdotal thinking or gut-level reactions that can lead them astray (Tversky and Kahneman, 1974).

In practice, we too often fall prey to two types of errors. First, we oversimplify the actual relationships and trends within data by either creating static snapshots that obscure the dynamics or showing only a small piece of the whole picture. At the other extreme, we create output that is so complex as to render it unusable by the individuals who rely on it as an aid in policymaking. Both situations can lead to significant errors in judgment and decision making and lead to the implementation of less-than-optimal policy.

To overcome these threats and keep our research and recommendations understandable while respecting the real complexity of the institution, we must become more creative in our thinking, analysis, and presentation. We illustrate our approach by addressing three sets of challenges, using enrollment management questions as examples. We stress that analyses and output generated should match the question posed, graphics should be used when possible to display complex information in simple and easily

NEW DIRECTIONS FOR INSTITUTIONAL RESEARCH, no. 137, Spring 2008 © Wiley Periodicals, Inc.
Published online in Wiley InterScience (www.interscience.wiley.com) • DOI: 10.1002/ir.239

71

understood formats, and even sophisticated analyses should yield simple and easily used results. Techniques range from simple layout or presentation formats in which the data provided more clearly address the question posed, to the design of easily used tools that present large volumes of data in simple and accessible formats, allowing even novice users to conduct statistical manipulations with the click of a button.

Challenge 1: Presenting Meaningful and Useful Information

Although routine descriptive reporting may seem simple, a thoughtful and creative approach to the presentation of results can make the difference between a report that sits on the shelf and a report that is used. There are many ways to format data summaries, perhaps the simplest and most frequently used being a table or bar graph displaying frequency distributions or percentages. Even within these simple forms of summary, however, many choices can be made that profoundly affect how useful the report will be.

To begin, we must determine what information to provide to the reader. This should start with consideration of the questions that the data or analyses are to answer. If the output created does not provide an answer to an important question, it should be omitted. Similarly, it is essential to know the audience, their level of sophistication, their familiarity with the subject matter, and the time that they will devote to understanding the report or analysis.

Results should be presented in a simple and clear manner. Superfluous digits should be dropped to keep the information clear, easy to understand, and easy to remember. Vertical lines, often unnecessary in tables, should be dropped. Any colors used should convey meaning rather than merely decorate. It is also essential that directional relationships be presented in the correct format so that the theorized direction of influence is clear.

We endorse seven basic principles explained in *Chicago Guide to Writing About Numbers* (Miller, 2004, p. 32):

1. Set the context for the numbers that you present through specifying the W's (who, what, when, where, why).
2. Choose effective examples and analogies. Use simple, familiar examples that your audience will be able to understand and relate to. Select contrasts that are realistic under real-world circumstances.
3. Choose vocabulary to suit your readers. Define terms and mention synonyms from related fields for statistical audiences. Replace jargon and mathematical symbols with colloquial language for nontechnical audiences.
4. Decide whether to present numbers in text, tables, or figures. Decide how many numbers you need to report. Estimate how much time your audience has to grasp your data. Assess whether your readers need exact values.
5. Report and interpret numbers in the text. Report them and specify their purpose. Interpret and relate them back to your main topic.

NEW DIRECTIONS FOR INSTITUTIONAL RESEARCH • DOI: 10.1002/ir

6. Specify both the direction and size of an association between variables. If a trend, is it rising or falling? If a difference across groups or places, which has the higher value and by how much?
7. To describe a pattern involving many numbers, summarize the overall pattern rather than repeating all the numbers. Find a generalization that fits most of the data. Report a few illustrative numbers from the associated table or chart. Describe exceptions to the general pattern.

We are also indebted to Edward Tufte who has produced four beautiful volumes about communicating with clarity and style, and highly recommend his work (Tufte, 1990, 1997, 2001, 2006).

Now, turning to a concrete example, suppose that we are to address the influence of gender as students apply for admission, are admitted or denied, pay an enrollment deposit, and finally register for courses. To summarize the effect of gender through this "enrollment funnel," we begin with a simple frequency distribution showing the total number of individuals at each point in the admissions cycle (Table 5.1). The information on the total number of males and females in each cell is useful data, and the basis for an answer to the question. However, merely presenting the raw data forces the reader to be responsible for doing the analysis.

The next obvious step is to provide the same data as percentages (Table 5.2). Although this makes clear the composition of the pool at each step of the process, it still fails to directly address the role of gender across the admissions cycle.

To address the issue directly, we must focus on the places where gender could make a difference. It is not in the number of students in each status but in the transitions from each status to the next. Table 5.3 is simple and clear: using far fewer digits than the previous efforts, it provides an answer to the question. Rather than focusing on raw data, it is oriented to the interesting processes.

Table 5.3 reveals gender differences in the rate of admission and in the "melt" from deposit to actual enrollment. A disproportionate number of female applicants are admitted relative to male applicants, and male applicants are more likely to melt, or fail to enroll after paying their enrollment deposit.

Table 5.1. Number of Applicants, Admits, Deposits, and Enrolled Students by Gender for One Academic Year

	Female	Male	Total
Apply	9,582	9,651	19,233
Admit	6,228	5,694	11,922
Deposit	2,989	2,676	5,665
Enroll	2,750	2,382	5,132

NEW DIRECTIONS FOR INSTITUTIONAL RESEARCH • DOI: 10.1002/ir

Table 5.2. Percentage of Applicants, Admits, Deposits, and Enrolled Students for each Gender for One Academic Year

	Female	Male	Total
Apply	50 percent	50 percent	100 percent
Admit	52	48	100
Deposit	53	47	100
Enroll	54	46	100

This example illustrates the importance of using the minimum number of cells to present the maximum amount of information to a reader. This also shows the need for output to match the question posed. In presenting findings for ease of use, the reader should not be required to perform additional computations or translations.

Challenge 2: Presenting Too Much Information

In spite of all efforts to simplify the information presented, there may still remain a large number of data that must be considered when making a decision. Consider the following situation: an institution wants to determine where top-quality applicants are coming from and assess where its recruitment efforts are underperforming in attracting applicants. In this case, the consumers will be not only high-level administrators but also ground-level recruiters who can combine their practical knowledge of territories with the data presented. These recruiters may not have significant experience in interpreting data, and so care must be given to how the data will be presented. A simple listing of where top-quality applicants have come from historically and whether those applicants were accepted into and attended the institution will lead to a large and impractical table containing far too much information to be of use in decision making. Figure 5.1 shows only the beginning of this unwieldy table.

From a high-level management viewpoint, this table is improved by aggregating the data by state and computing yield rates. However the table is still difficult to interpret simply due to its size (see Table 5.4). In this case, at least two values need to be compared simultaneously to reach a valuable

Table 5.3. Effects of Gender on Admit, Deposit, and Enrollment Rates

	Female	Male
Admit rate	65 percent	59 percent
Deposit rate (from admits)	48	47
Enrollment rate (from deposits)	92	89

Figure 5.1. Applicants, Admits, and Enrolled Students by Geographical Location

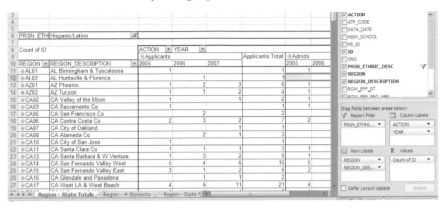

conclusion: how many students are interested in our institution (applications) and how many of these students actually enroll (yield). The numbers of offers of admission and enrolled students are also of interest. Sorting the table by relevant characteristics could improve its ability to communicate, but it is still too large to be readily used by administrators.

Table 5.4. Number of Applicants, Admits, and Enrolled Students and Yield Rate by Home State

State	Applications			Offers of Admission			Enrolled			Admit to Enrolled Yield
	2005	2006	2007	2005	2006	2007	2005	2006	2007	
Illinois	839	888	1439	820	853	1,367	145	230	377	26%
Indiana	1,141	1,120	1,313	1,118	1,094	1,289	497	523	608	46
Ohio	252	286	330	247	284	316	45	48	79	24
New York	169	207	265	165	194	253	21	32	36	14
Missouri	77	119	177	76	114	171	20	34	55	31
California	135	132	153	133	129	140	16	22	26	17
Michigan	102	109	137	101	106	131	19	21	29	21
Texas	101	78	125	97	75	115	20	18	21	17
Kentucky	84	75	118	83	74	111	15	19	23	19
New Jersey	90	88	118	89	88	110	11	19	17	14
. . .	. . .	. . .	. . .	. . .	. . .	. . .	. . .	. . .	. . .	. . .
Maryland	66	87	79	64	86	76	12	15	11	14
Florida	41	47	70	40	46	66	5	9	12	17
Georgia	41	50	69	41	50	67	9	7	18	26
Wisconsin	30	34	64	30	32	59	6	6	15	23
Minnesota	31	44	61	29	42	52	9	5	13	21
Pennsylvania	42	42	60	38	42	57	11	9	13	22
Massachusetts	47	50	53	43	50	50	3	12	10	19
Connecticut	29	40	51	28	36	43	7	6	8	16
Virginia	40	45	51	40	43	48	11	8	16	31

In instances such as this, the data are much more easily captured using a picture- or graph-based representation such as the one in Figure 5.2. This was created using a simple, inexpensive mapping program. More sophisticated geographic information system (GIS) software requires more time to learn, but is much more powerful. Figure 5.2 shows a map of the United States with states shaded by their admissions yield rates, and with dots sized to represent the number of high-quality applications. Within this display, it is easy to see which states produce a number of high-quality applicants yet have low yield rates (for example, New York) and which states have high yield rates yet are producing a low number of high-quality applicants (such as Nebraska). Maps can be sized interactively to reveal more detail appropriate to recruiters who are concerned with results within their own territories or to higher-level managers concerned with the big picture.

In deciding when it is best to use a graph or map rather than a table, consideration should be given to how the information will be used. Again, only information relevant to the question being asked should be provided. Economy and simplicity remain the keys to clear communication. And of course tables plus graphs or maps can often be the combination approach that delivers the big picture as well as some fine detail.

Displaying large, complex data sets can also be made simpler through the use of color. For another example, consider an institution interested in adjusting its admissions standards based on the performance of past students, with performance measured in terms of grade point average and graduation rate.

Figure 5.3 shows the mean and standard deviation of grade point average and graduation rate for each level of admissions test and essay score, raw output that is essentially useless to anyone but the analyst.

Figure 5.2. Graphical Representation of the Number of Applicants and Yield Rate for Each U.S. State

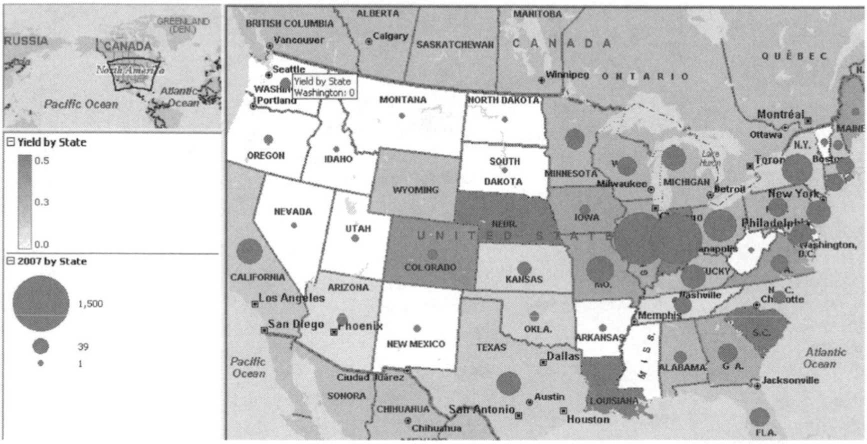

Figure 5.3. Screen Shot of Output Containing Average GPAs for All Levels of SAT and Admissions Essay Score Performance

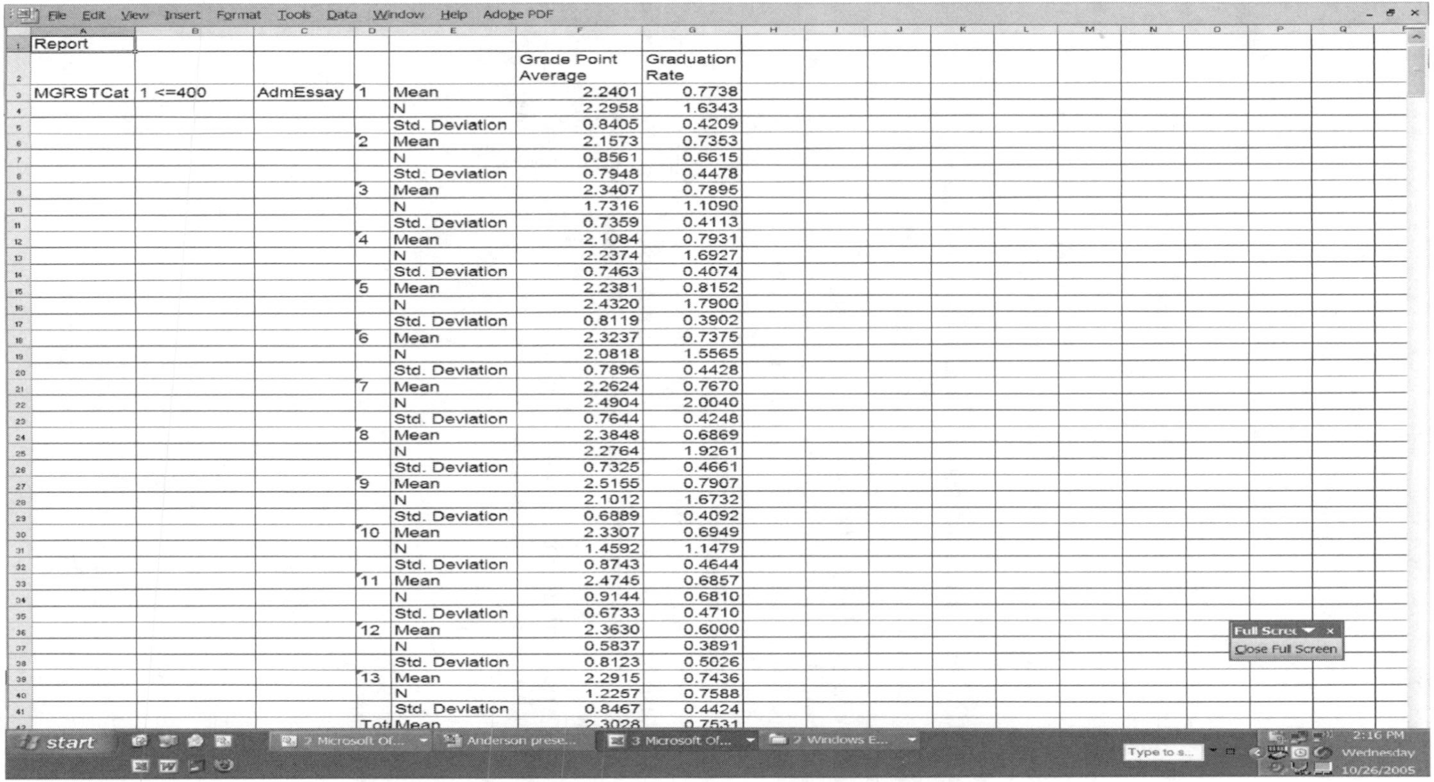

MGRSTCat 1 <=400

AdmEssay		Grade Point Average	Graduation Rate
1	Mean	2.2401	0.7738
	N	2.2958	1.6343
	Std. Deviation	0.8405	0.4209
2	Mean	2.1673	0.7353
	N	0.8561	0.6615
	Std. Deviation	0.7948	0.4478
3	Mean	2.3407	0.7895
	N	1.7316	1.1090
	Std. Deviation	0.7359	0.4113
4	Mean	2.1084	0.7931
	N	2.2374	1.6927
	Std. Deviation	0.7463	0.4074
5	Mean	2.2381	0.8152
	N	2.4320	1.7900
	Std. Deviation	0.8119	0.3902
6	Mean	2.3237	0.7375
	N	2.0818	1.5565
	Std. Deviation	0.7896	0.4428
7	Mean	2.2624	0.7670
	N	2.4904	2.0040
	Std. Deviation	0.7644	0.4248
8	Mean	2.3848	0.6869
	N	2.2764	1.9261
	Std. Deviation	0.7325	0.4661
9	Mean	2.5155	0.7907
	N	2.1012	1.6732
	Std. Deviation	0.6889	0.4092
10	Mean	2.3307	0.6949
	N	1.4592	1.1479
	Std. Deviation	0.8743	0.4644
11	Mean	2.4745	0.6857
	N	0.9144	0.6810
	Std. Deviation	0.6733	0.4710
12	Mean	2.3630	0.6000
	N	0.5837	0.3891
	Std. Deviation	0.8123	0.5026
13	Mean	2.2915	0.7436
	N	1.2257	0.7588
	Std. Deviation	0.8467	0.4424
Tot	Mean	2.3028	0.7531

This information is more usefully arranged in a table with rows for test score categories and columns for essay score categories (Table 5.5). This begins to be comprehensible, but remains of limited value for busy policymakers who cannot quickly discern the important patterns in the data.

By adding meaningful color gradients to this table, as shown in Table 5.6, the trends within the data become immediately clear, and the table is suddenly usable. Students most likely to achieve a high first-semester college GPA (green shading in practice, white for publication here) can be easily identified, as can those students likely to achieve a low first-semester college GPA (red shading in practice, dark gray for publication here). Shading to bring out meaning in tables is very easy to accomplish in modern spreadsheets using conditional formatting, as well as even coloring cells individually to highlight values of greatest interest.

Challenge 3: Presenting Dynamic Information

Policymakers often want to determine how changes in policy would affect multiple goals simultaneously. For example, an institution might consider the impact of various levels of scholarship funding to specific groups of students on class size, quality, diversity, retention, and the budget. This can lead to very complex output regarding how each level of change would affect each goal individually. This output is often extensive and difficult to understand without advanced statistical training and a substantial investment of time to examine the tables and regression equations generated.

Displaying this information in a format that is simple yet does not compromise the richness of the analysis is a challenge. To provide a comprehensive set of static tables would be overwhelming. To present a single simple table would fail to communicate enough detail to support sound decisions. The solution is a dynamic table that displays a comprehensible view of the outcomes of one possible policy at a time, with controls to allow the viewer to explore other options (see Figure 5.4). Behind the scenes, hidden on other tabs, are the results of a broad range of simulations based on regression analysis. Users simply manipulate the arrows to increase and decrease scholarship amounts for five of the six groups of students. As the scholarship amounts change, the results of the relevant simulations appear. Within a spreadsheet engine such as this, end users can easily see how policy changes will affect the outcomes. Policymakers balance their priorities based on all the relevant data. What would otherwise be an overwhelming and time-consuming task is now accomplished quickly and easily.

Similarly, when admissions standards and how those admissions standards will affect the size, quality, and composition of an enrolled class are being considered, a complex set of data and analyses is needed. But any set of static tables produced would either oversimplify the problem or be too lengthy and cumbersome to use and interpret. As researchers, we know that

Table 5.5. Average GPAs for All Levels of SAT Performance by All Levels of Admissions Essay Score Performance

SAT Range	Admissions Essay Score												
	1	2	3	4	5	6	7	8	9	10	11	12	13
400 or below	2.2	2.2	2.3	2.1	2.2	2.3	2.3	2.4	2.5	2.3	2.5	2.4	2.3
410–500	2.2	2.2	2.5	2.1	2.4	2.3	2.3	2.5	2.5	2.7	2.8	2.9	2.6
510–600	2.1	2.6	2.4	2.5	2.4	2.4	2.5	2.6	2.7	2.7	2.8	3	2.7
610–700	2.5	2.4	2.5	2.5	2.5	2.5	2.6	2.7	2.7	2.8	2.9	3	2.7
710–800	2.5	2.5	2.5	2.5	2.5	2.5	2.7	2.6	2.8	2.8	2.9	3.1	2.9
810–900	2.3	2.5	2.6	2.5	2.6	2.6	2.6	2.8	2.8	2.9	3	3.1	3
910–1000	2.6	2.6	2.6	2.7	2.6	2.6	2.8	2.9	2.9	3	3.1	3.2	3.1
1010–1100	2.4	2.5	2.6	2.6	2.7	2.8	2.8	2.9	2.9	3	3.2	3.2	3.1
1110–1200	2.8	2.2	2.8	2.8	2.9	2.9	2.8	2.9	3	3	3.2	3.3	3.3
1210–1300	2.4	2.7	2.5	2.7	3	2.8	2.9	2.8	3	3	3.3	3.4	3.4
1310–1400	2.9	3.1	2.7	2.4	2.9	2.6	2.8	3.1	3.1	3.2	3.3	3.4	3.5
1410–1500	1.9	1.5	2.8	1.9	2.7	2.5	3.1	2.7	3	3.3	3.3	3.5	3.6
1510–1600	2.7	2.8	3.3	3.1	2.7	2.7	2.7	3.2	3.3	3	3.5	3.6	3.7

more variables included in an analysis make it more complicated to display the results. By presenting this information as a simulation using a spreadsheet, the end user deals only with inputs and outputs; the actual engine of the analysis is hidden. In the spreadsheet shown in Figure 5.5, the end user can change admission standards through the use of a switch (in this exam-

Table 5.6. Color-Coded Average GPAs for All Levels of SAT Score by All Levels of Admissions Essay Score

SAT Range	Admissions Essay Score												
	1	2	3	4	5	6	7	8	9	10	11	12	13
400 or below	2.2	2.2	2.3	2.1	2.2	2.3	2.3	2.4	2.5	2.3	2.5	2.4	2.3
410–500	2.2	2.2	2.5	2.1	2.4	2.3	2.3	2.5	2.5	2.7	2.8	2.9	2.6
510–600	2.1	2.6	2.4	2.5	2.4	2.4	2.5	2.6	2.7	2.7	2.8	3	2.7
610–700	2.5	2.4	2.5	2.5	2.5	2.5	2.6	2.7	2.7	2.8	2.9	3	2.7
710–800	2.5	2.5	2.5	2.5	2.5	2.5	2.7	2.6	2.8	2.8	2.9	3.1	2.9
810–900	2.3	2.5	2.6	2.5	2.6	2.6	2.6	2.8	2.8	2.9	3	3.1	3
910–1000	2.6	2.6	2.6	2.7	2.6	2.6	2.8	2.9	2.9	3	3.1	3.2	3.1
1010–1100	2.4	2.5	2.6	2.6	2.7	2.8	2.8	2.9	2.9	3	3.2	3.2	3.1
1110–1200	2.8	2.2	2.8	2.8	2.9	2.9	2.8	2.9	3	3	3.2	3.3	3.3
1210–1300	2.4	2.7	2.5	2.7	3	2.8	2.9	2.8	3	3	3.3	3.4	3.4
1310–1400	2.9	3.1	2.7	2.4	2.9	2.6	2.8	3.1	3.1	3.2	3.3	3.4	3.5
1410–1500	1.9	1.5	2.8	1.9	2.7	2.5	3.1	2.7	3	3.3	3.3	3.5	3.6
1510–1600	2.7	2.8	3.3	3.1	2.7	2.7	2.7	3.2	3.3	3	3.5	3.6	3.7

Figure 5.4. Screen Shot Showing an Example Spreadsheet Engine in Which Funding Amounts Can Be Varied by the End User to Determine the Effect on Enrollment, Tuition Revenue, and Average SAT Score

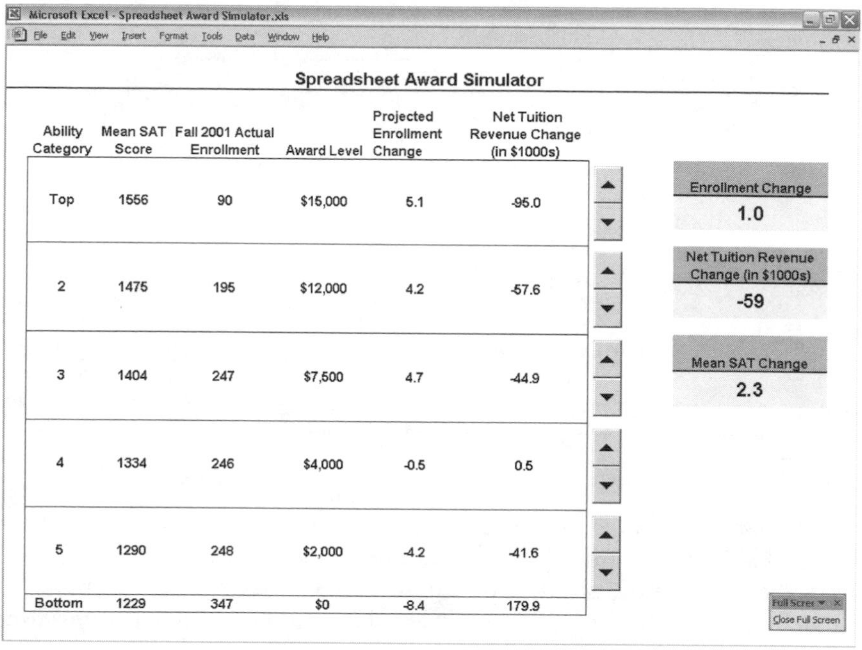

Ability Category	Mean SAT Score	Fall 2001 Actual Enrollment	Award Level	Projected Enrollment Change	Net Tuition Revenue Change (in $1000s)
Top	1556	90	$15,000	5.1	-95.0
2	1475	195	$12,000	4.2	-57.6
3	1404	247	$7,500	4.7	-44.9
4	1334	246	$4,000	-0.5	0.5
5	1290	248	$2,000	-4.2	-41.6
Bottom	1229	347	$0	-8.4	179.9

ple, a spreadsheet feature called a spin button) to determine how changes in admission standards across groups will affect the outcomes. Similarly, growth rates in the applicant pool can be simulated in the lower portion of the table.

Conclusion

Institutional research professionals frequently work within an environment that is rich in complex operational data. Policymakers aspire to be data-driven managers through the use of tables and summaries provided by the institutional research professional. To allow policymakers to achieve this goal, institutional research professionals must be clear, concise, and creative in displaying information.

To achieve effective presentation, we advocate a reflective focus on what information is necessary. Only this necessary information should be displayed, and in a simple, uncluttered format. The information provided should directly answer the questions at hand. Appropriate presentation strategies must be selected that make the best use of the data available and

Figure 5.5. Example Spreadsheet Engine in Which Admissions Standards Can Be Varied by the End User to Determine the Effect on Enrollment and Related Statistics by Residency and Ethnicity

Simulated Effects of Proposed Admissions Standards

Minority Demographics

Residents	Existing	Proposed	Difference		African Americans Existing	Proposed	Difference	Hispanics Existing	Proposed	Difference	All Others Existing	Proposed	Difference
Applicants	10,575	10,575	-	Adjust Resident Admission Standard Here	641	641	-	277	277	-	9,657	9,657	-
Admits	7,418	5,195	(2,223)		313	129	(184)	190	106	(84)	6,914	4,960	(1,95
Deposits	3,994	2,713	(1,281)		133	55	(78)	98	55	(43)	3,762	2,602	(1,16
Enrolled	4,393	2,537	(1,856)		321	51	(270)	108	51	(55)	3,926	2,419	(1,50
Mean SAT	1093	1202	109		929	1159	230	1046	1172	127	1105	1204	9

Non-residents	Existing	Proposed	Difference		African Americans Existing	Proposed	Difference	Hispanics Existing	Proposed	Difference	All Others Existing	Proposed	Difference
Applicants	16,903	16,903	-	Adjust Non-Resident Admission Standard Here	363	383	-	516	516	-	16,024	16,024	-
Admits	12,226	14,745	2,519		215	216	1	382	418	36	11,827	14,111	2,48
Deposits	3,482	4,377	915		42	52	10	75	84	9	3,344	4,276	93
Enrolled	2,860	3,594	734		36	43	7	61	68	7	2,721	3,489	768
Mean SAT	1182	1179	(3)		1036	1079	44	1138	1121	(17)	1187	1182	(
TOTAL ENROLLMENT	7,253	6,131	(1,122)		357	94	(263)	187	119	(48)	6,847	5,908	(73
% Enrolled Non-residents	39%	59%	19%		10%	45%	35%	37%	71%	34%	41%	59%	18
%Enrolled Each Demographic					4.92%	1.53%	-3.39%	2.30%	1.95%	-0.35%	91.64%	96.35%	4.71

Simulated Effects of Inflation

Residents	Existing	Proposed	Difference		African Americans Existing	Proposed	Difference	Hispanics Existing	Proposed	Difference	All Others Existing	Proposed	Difference
Applicants	10,575	11,104	529	Adjust Resident Inflation Here	641	673	32	277	291	14	9,657	10,140	48
Admits	7,418	5,455	(1,963)		313	135	(178)	190	111	(79)	6,914	5,208	(1,70
Deposits	3,994	2,848	(1,146)		133	58	(75)	98	54	(40)	3,762	2,733	(1,02
Enrolled	4,393	2,664	(1,729)		321	54	(267)	108	54	(52)	3,926	2,540	(1,38
Mean SAT	1093	1202	109		929	1159	230	1046	1172	127	1105	1204	9

Non-residents	Existing	Proposed	Difference		African Americans Existing	Proposed	Difference	Hispanics Existing	Proposed	Difference	All Others Existing	Proposed	Difference
Applicants	16,903	18,424	1,521	Adjust Non-Resident Inflation Here	363	396	33	516	562	46	16,024	17,468	1,44
Admits	12,226	16,072	3,846		215	235	20	382	456	74	11,827	15,381	3,75
Deposits	3,482	4,771	1,309		42	57	15	75	92	17	3,344	4,661	1,31
Enrolled	2,860	3,918	1,058		36	46	10	61	75	14	2,721	3,803	1,08
Mean SAT	1182	1179	(3)		1036	1079	44	1138	1121	(17)	1187	1182	(
TOTAL ENROLLMENT	7,253	6,582	(671)		357	100	(257)	166	128	(38)	6,847	6,343	(30
% Enrolled Non-residents	39%	60%	20%		10%	48%	38%	37%	59%	21%	41%	60%	19
%Enrolled Each Demographic					4.92%	1.53%	-3.40%	2.29%	1.95%	-0.34%	91.64%	96.37%	4.73

present them with an appropriate level of complexity while maintaining comprehensibility. Often, displaying needed information in a simple and easily used manner requires creativity in presentation. New technology and tools can be valuable in these efforts. Beyond tables, graphs, maps, color, and dynamic simulations can provide effective and simple ways of communicating rich and complex information.

References

Miller, J. *The Chicago Guide to Writing About Numbers: The Effective Presentation of Quantitative Information.* Chicago: University of Chicago Press, 2004.

Tufte, E. *Envisioning Information.* Cheshire, Conn.: Graphics Press, 1990.

Tufte, E. *Visual Explanations: Images and Quantities, Evidence and Narrative.* Cheshire, Conn.: Graphics Press, 1997.

NEW DIRECTIONS FOR INSTITUTIONAL RESEARCH • DOI: 10.1002/ir

Tufte, E. *The Visual Display of Quantitative Information* (2nd ed.). Cheshire, Conn.: Graphics Press, 2001.

Tufte, E. *Beautiful Evidence.* Cheshire, Conn.: Graphics Press, 2006.

Tversky, A., and Kahneman, D. "Judgment Under Uncertainty: Heuristics and Biases." *Science,* 1974, *185,* 1124–1131.

DOUGLAS K. ANDERSON *is director of enrollment planning and research in the office of enrollment management at Indiana University, Bloomington.*

BRIDGETT J. MILNER *is assistant director of enrollment planning and research in the office of enrollment management at Indiana University, Bloomington.*

CHRIS J. FOLEY *is director of admissions at Indiana University-Purdue University Indianapolis.*

6

Bayesian network is introduced and illustrated as a flexible and reliable data analytical technique for extracting useful information from large-scale institutional databases.

Bayesian Modeling in Institutional Research: An Example of Nonlinear Classification

Yonghong Jade Xu, Terry T. Ishitani

One of the primary functions of institutional research is to provide institutional stakeholders with critical data and strategic support needed in their policymaking and decision-making process. Colleges and universities have been challenged by a wide range of educational agendas, and many of these agendas require institutional researchers to analyze sizable data with a great deal of elaborations. Which methodological approach is more appropriate: qualitative or quantitative, or perhaps both? What are the most effective ways to present study findings to the university community? Although answers to such questions vary substantially depending on the agendas, producing "better information faster" (Ferren and Aylesworth, 2001) is always expected. In the past, the educational research community suffered from not being able to handle large data sets in analytical research because of limited computing technology. In recent years, though, rapid advancement has taken place in computing technology that allows institutional researchers to efficiently and effectively address data of increasing volume and structural complexity (Luan, 2002). In this chapter, we propose a new data analytical technique, Bayesian belief networks (BBN), to add to the toolbox for institutional research.

BBN is a Bayesian probabilistic approach to nonlinear classification problems that is applicable to situations in which large numbers of data are available, expert inputs may be used in addition to the objective information

in the data, a large number of qualitative and quantitative variables have potential impact, and the nature of the analysis is exploratory and, most likely, explanatory (Elder and Pregibon, 1996; Heckerman, 1997). Examples of such problems include identifying factors related to effective student retention, investigating factors contributing to faculty turnover, and pinpointing critical parameters in classifying peer institutions. We discuss the advantages of BBN in comparison to conventional statistical procedures that were developed prior to the 1970s for hypothesis-based analyses, and later exemplify an application of BBN by analyzing a database and classifying a national sample of faculty members to the right Carnegie type of their institution.

Introduction to Bayesian Belief Networks

In comparison to parametric procedures in classical statistics, BBN has several advantages for exploratory analysis of large data sets. First, all variables are treated as nominal measures. Interval and ratio variables are included by binning the continuous values into a number of discrete intervals. Binning of continuous variables makes the BBN analysis robust against noisy data, irregular distributions, and loose data structure. This robustness is especially useful when researchers have to analyze observational data from convenient or opportunistic samples or that constitute the population (Hand, 1999; Hand, Mannila, and Smyth, 2001). Second, having only nominal variables, BBN measures variable relationships by the level of association and uses threshold values to replace hypothesis testing in data analysis. Level of association is a better approach to measure nonlinear relationships between variables. In addition, the use of "threshold" makes BBN a more flexible alternative to classical statistics when working with a large sample size because oversensitivity to minor differences in significance tests is avoided and distributional assumptions (for example, normality and homogeneity of variance) are no longer necessary. Furthermore, minimal use of significant tests enables proper handling of hierarchical variable relationships, such as variables at the individual nested within institutional levels, in a BBN model given that the threats from correlated error terms are out of the question.

Third, large data sets often contain not only a large number of observations (sample size) but also a large number of variables (high dimensionality). In classic statistics, a confirmatory approach is common in which the functional form of the model (such as regression analysis and AVOVA) is assumingly known and the analysis is to make the best estimate of the model parameters for statistical inferences. However, data of high dimensionality often mean it is infeasible to select variables and determine the model a priori. Rather than predefining a model structure, BBN explores the model space and searches for the optimal model from a set of competing and admissible models (Pednault, 1999). Theoretically any subset of input variables can form one or more potential models, which means the model space consists of candidate models of substantially different structures. In the automated search for a BBN of optimal accuracy, numerous candidate models are tried and compared. The process of model construction is exploratory rather than confirmatory, and the final model, the one with the best accuracy, is eventually "discovered" and presented.

Fourth, findings of the BBN analysis are presented in a graph that depicts the variable relationships in a network structure. The graphic display makes the model presentation intuitive and informative for exploratory purpose and is more "natural" in comparison to the mathematical models produced by most statistical procedures. Although classification with nominal variables can also be performed statistically using decision tree analysis and statisticians have found that Bayesian networks and decision trees have about the same classification accuracy (Singh and Provan, 1995), BBN considers the dependencies between the input variables and allows a more complete account of uncertainty than do decision trees (Western, 1999). The dependencies among input variables also increase the power of handling missing data in BBN analysis (Heckerman, 1997).

Finally, in a BBN model, estimation of the model parameter, the posterior probabilities, is based on the joint probabilities that connect the input variables to the outcome variable. For any combination of the input values, the posterior distribution of the outcome variable is presented as a probabilistic variable that explicitly expresses the estimation uncertainty (Western, 1999). This is a conceptual difference between BBN and classical statistics. Unlike classical statistics that consider model parameters as fixed but unknown population values and express estimation uncertainty implicitly with standard errors, BBN treats the model parameters as random variables rather than single values.

Foundation of Bayesian Belief Networks

The foundation of BBN is Bayes's theorem, a set of probability rules derived by Thomas Bayes in the 1760s. The basic version of Bayes's theorem starts with the product rule for independent events:

$$p(AB) = p(A)\, p(B) \tag{1}$$

where $p(AB)$ means the probability of A and B happening together. The rule is a special case of the following product rule for dependent events, where $p(A|B)$ means the probability of A given that B has already occurred:

$$p(AB) = p(A)\, p(B|A) \text{ and} \tag{2}$$

$$p(AB) = p(B)\, p(A|B) \tag{3}$$

Combining equations 2 and 3, we get

$$p(A)\, p(B|A) = p(B)\, p(A|B),$$

so Bayes's theorem can be given as

$$p(A|B) = \frac{p(A)p(B|A)}{p(B)} \qquad (4)$$

which provides the probability of event A happening given that event B has happened, calculated in terms of other known probabilities (Cumming, 2003; Western, 1999).

Bayes's theorem can be extended to chain more probabilities together. For instance, suppose that we need to calculate p(AB) given that a third event, I, has happened. Written as p(AB|I), with the product rule (equations 2 and 3), we have:

$$p(AB|I) = p(B|I)\ p(A|BI)\ \text{and}$$

$$p(AB|I) = p(A|I)\ p(B|AI) \qquad (5)$$

Therefore, Bayes's rule becomes:

$$p(A|BI) = \frac{p(A|I)p(B|AI)}{p(B|I)} \qquad (6)$$

which gives the probability of event A happening given that event B and event I have happened. If A stands for the outcome event X, B for evidence E, and I for context C, equation 6 can be written as:

$$p(X|EC) = \frac{p(X|C)p(E|XC)}{p(E|C)} \qquad (7)$$

where $p(X|EC)$ is the probability of X given Evidence E in Context C.

If more variables are involved, the chained Bayes's theorem becomes very complex with a large number of intercorrelated events (variables) and their conditional probabilities (Gillies, 2001; Winkler, 1972). When these events and their conditional probabilities are encoded in a treelike network, the resulted graphical model is called BBN.

Three important concepts in the discussion of BBN are prior probability, degree of belief, and posterior probability. Prior probability, $p(A)$, is the probability of event A regardless of the evidence. In Bayesian statistics, $p(A)$ can be obtained empirically from sample data using the probability sum rule, or it can be estimated by experts as a subjective probability (Western, 1999). Prior probabilities, as the gateway to including subjective inputs from domain experts for predicting future outcomes, is a distinctive feature that makes Bayesian probability different from classical probability. Bayesian statisticians perceive probabilities as degrees of belief that can be assessed by a person and updated with new empirical evidence. However, a majority of classical statisticians regard nonsample-based prior probabilities as arbitrary and frown on the inclusion of subjective human judgment in mathematical models. Be it empirical or subjective, the prior probability $p(A)$ can be updated when new evidence E becomes available, and the updated probability is called *posterior probability* $p(A|EC)$. As summarized by Western (1999), Bayesian analysis is to update prior beliefs "with sample data using Bayes['s] rule to obtain posterior probability statement about unknown quantities" (p. 31).

A BBN Example

BBN is a powerful tool for exploratory research not only because the algorithms are mathematically sound, but also because the networks have an intuitive graphical representation. The model is expressed as a diagram wherein variables are nodes, their relationships (causal or dependent) are shown as a set of directed arcs, and a conditional probability table is attached to each variable (Winkler, 1972).

An example can help explain BBN and illustrate its applications in higher education research. Assume that institutional decision makers are initiating changes in faculty-related policies as part of the effort to move the institution up in the Carnegie Classification. A Bayesian analysis can help to answer questions such as what factors distinctively shape the work experience of faculty in different types of institutions.

For demonstration purposes, we use the survey results of the National Study of Postsecondary Faculty (NSOPF:04) sponsored by the National Center of Educational Statistics (NCES). The NSOPF survey had a two-stage stratified design and began data collection from a nationally representative sample of approximately 1,070 postsecondary institutions and more than 34,300 individuals employed at these institutions. In the faculty survey, respondents were asked extensively about their teaching, research, services at work, and demographic information. Over 26,100 faculty and instructional staff completed the survey, for a 76 percent weighted response rate. In the institution survey, data were collected about the makeup of faculty workforce and other financial and benefit information. In addition, NCES provided institutional data that includes student enrollment, student and faculty full-time equivalents (FTEs), institutional expenditures, and geographical location. We kept both faculty and institutional variables in the analysis for two reasons: (1) institutional factors not only influence Carnegie Classification, but also have substantial impact on faculty work experience, and (2) they are needed in order to show how BBN handles hierarchical data structure. Because of the stratified sampling of NSOPF:04, the data were weighted in the analysis.

Variable Selection. The literature indicates that institutions of different types commit to different missions and have different expectations and reward systems for faculty teaching, research, and services (see, for example, Hall, 1995). In the NSOPF data, a variety of measures of institutional characteristics and faculty teaching, research, and service activities are available. However, some of the measures are highly correlated with each other, and it is difficult to decide which variables to keep and which to discard. Knowing that BBN has the power to explore myriad sources of uncertainty, we decided to keep a relatively large number of variables in the analysis. As shown in Table 6.1, forty-three variables were used in the analysis; twenty-seven of them are at the individual faculty level and sixteen at the institutional level. Although BBN can be used for prediction, we call predictor and predicted variables input and outcome variables, respectively, to emphasize the classification nature of this analysis.

Variable Transformation. In principle, nonlinear Bayesian statistics estimate the posterior probabilities based on the joint probabilities of the input nominal variables (Winkler, 1972). All variables need to have discrete values in order to define a finite product state space that consists of all unique combinations of the input variable values. To meet this requirement, we had to group every continuous variable into category-like intervals or bins (Cheng and Greiner, 1999). A continuous variable can be converted into intervals of equal width or intervals of equal probability. In our example, we determined the number of intervals for every continuous variable based on its distribution and tried to keep the same number of observations in each interval. This approximation to a uniform distribution (in other words, the chances are equal for respondents to fall into each interval) simplified the estimate of prior probability and reduced the computational complexity (Pearl, 1995; Heckerman, 1997). Information on binning of continuous variables is available in Table 6.1.

Data Analysis. Statistical analysis in its classical sense usually means estimating parameters of a prespecified model structure such as multiple regression or analysis of variance from sample data (Hand, Mannila, and Smyth, 2001; Pednault, 1999). In BBN analysis, however, it may not be realistic to predetermine the model structure when the number of input variables is large and their relationships to each other are unclear. Imagine that any random combination of the input variables could be a functional structure of the model; all potential model structures collectively form the "model space." Implementing a BBN therefore consists of two major tasks. First, the functional structure of a best-fit model must be identified from the model space; second, the parameters (posterior probability) of the functional model need to be estimated (Cheng and Greiner, 1999; Heckerman, 1999).

In our example, learning the functional structure of the BBN model is to identify the personal and institutional factors that classify faculty members into the type of institutions they are employed at and determine how the factors are related in the model of best classification accuracy. Ideally,

Table 6.1. Variables Included in the BBN Analysis

Variables	Name	Note
Individual level		
Employed full or part time at this institution	Q5	1 = Full time; 2 = Part time
Rank	Q10	1 = Professor; 2 = Associate professor; 3 = Assistant professor; 4 = Instructor; 5 = Lecturer; 6 = Other title
Tenure status	Q12	1 = Tenured; 2 = On tenure track but not tenured 3 = Not on tenure track 4 = Not tenured because institution had no tenure system
Highest degree	Q17A1	1 = Doctoral 2 = 1st-professional 3 = Master of Fine Arts/Social Work 4 = Other master's degree
Percent time spent on instruction, undergraduate	Q32A	Binned: 4 intervals
Percent time spent on instruction, graduate/first-professional	Q32B	Binned: 4 intervals
Percent time spent on research activities	Q32C	Binned: 3 intervals
Percent time spent on other unspecified activities	Q32D	Binned: 3 intervals
Serve on thesis/dissertation committees	Q48	0 = No; 1 = Yes
Hours per week, administrative committees	Q49	Binned: 3 intervals
Career articles, refereed journals	Q52AA	Binned: 4 intervals
Career articles, nonrefereed journals	Q52AB	Binned: 3 intervals
Career book reviews, chapters, creative works	Q52AC	Binned: 3 intervals
Career exhibitions, performances	Q52AF	Binned: 2 intervals
Career patents, computer software	Q52AG	0 = No; 1 = Yes
Scholarly activity, any funded	Q55	0 = No; 1 = Yes

(continued)

Table 6.1.   (continued)

Variables	Name	Note
Amount of income from basic salary from institution	Q66A	Binned: 5 intervals
Gender	Q71	1 = Male; 2 = Female
Citizenship status	Q81	0 = No; 1 = Yes
Total student credit hours in classes	X04Q37	Binned: 4 intervals
Total classroom credit hours in classes, undergraduate	X13Q37	Binned: 3 intervals
Total classroom credit hours in classes, grad/first-professional	X14Q37	Binned: 3 intervals
Technology index	X01Q39	0 = Use neither websites/e-mail 1 = Use e-mail, not websites 2 = Use websites, not e-mail 3 = Use both websites/e-mail
Recent total publications/scholarly works	X02Q52	Binned: 3 intervals
Race/ethnicity recoded	X03Q74	1 = American Indian/Alaska Native 2 = Asian/Pacific Islander 3 = Black/African American non-Hispanic 4 = Hispanic White or Hispanic Black 5 = White non-Hispanic
Institutional level		
Ratio of FTE enrollment/FTE faculty	X10Q0	Binned: 5 intervals
Enrollment FTE, undergraduate	X13Q0	Binned: 5 intervals
Enrollment FTE, first-professional and graduate	GradFTE	Binned: 3 intervals
Enrollment minority percentage	Minority	Binned: 3 intervals
Core expenses, percentage on instruction	InstPct	Binned: 4 intervals
Core expenses, percentage on research activities	ResPct	Binned: 4 intervals
Core expenses, total (in 1000s)	X35Q0	Binned: 4 intervals
Number faculty on institution faculty list	FACTOTAL	Binned: 4 intervals
Number full-time faculty, fall 2003, reported	I1A	Binned: 4 intervals
Full-time tenure: number considered for tenure, 2002–03	I4	Binned: 2 intervals

(continued)

Table 6.1.   (continued)

Variables	Name	Note
Ratio of faculty tenured to faculty considered for tenure	TNRatio	Binned: 3 intervals
Full-time faculty: union representation	I12	0 = No; 1 = Yes
Undergraduate instruction: percent full-time faculty	I19A	Binned: 4 intervals
Undergraduate instruction: percent part-time faculty	I19B	Binned: 4 intervals
Ratio of part-time to full-time faculty members	PtFtRt	Binned: 3 intervals
2000 Carnegie code, 7 category (outcome variable)	X106Q0	1 = Doctoral-Extensive 2 = Doctoral-Intensive 3 = Medical 4 = Master's 5 = Baccalaureate 6 = Associate 7 = Other

a full joint probability distribution over the entire product state space of all variables must be constructed in order to identify the model of best accuracy (Winkler, 1972). However, this task is practically impossible because there are forty-three variables in the analysis, and the computational difficulty increases exponentially with the number of variables in Bayesian network learning. Rather than doing an exhaustive search in the model space, Bayesian statisticians have to make acceptable compromises, such as searching for the optimal model from a subset of candidate models selected randomly in the model space or reducing the number of input variables algorithmically (Niedermayer, 1998). The Bayesian software that we used, Belief Network Powersoft, reduces the computational requirement by using a threshold value (user selected or system determined) to drop variables that have only "weak" relationships with others from subsequent analysis (Cheng and Greiner, 1999).

Demonstrating an exploratory study, we decided to build an empirical BBN where we specified no prior probabilities subjectively and let the software learn the model entirely from the data. Thus, once the data were preprocessed and entered, the learning of a BBN model was virtually an automated process. We needed only to experiment with different threshold values, with each value producing an admissible BBN model. Selected from those competing admissible models, the final model should have a relatively parsimonious structure and high prediction accuracy.

Interpretation of the BBN Model

A few BBN models were produced after we tried different threshold values. Information on four of the competing models is summarized in Table 6.2, and the network structure of one of the four models is illustrated in Figure 6.1 (the conditional probability tables are omitted due to space limitations). To select the optimal final model, a balance between classification accuracy and structural simplicity is advised. Classification accuracy is measured as the percentage of cases or observations that are classified into the correct outcome category. The better a model fits the data set, the more accurate the classifications are said to be. However, when high accuracies are companied by a large number of variables (nodes) and too many conditional dependencies (arcs), this may be a sign of model overfit, meaning that the model works well only with the data set used to build the model and may not be accurate for new data sets (Cheng and others, 2001).

Visual examination of the graphical network is an opportunity to evaluate intuitively the model simplicity. A rough numerical index is the ratio between the number of arcs and number of nodes. The model may be too complex when the ratio is greater than 2. On the other hand, a ratio close to 1 could mean model underfit: important conditional dependencies are missing, and the prediction accuracies are poor.

Comparisons and evaluation of the four models in Table 6.2 result in a final model produced at the threshold value ten times the default system value. This model consists of thirteen input variables and classifies 88.43 percent faculty members accurately to the Carnegie institutional type of their institutions (the output variable). As shown in Figure 6.1, ten of the thirteen variables have a direct impact on the faculty classification to different institutional types: (1) ratio of student FTE enrollment to faculty FTE, (2) undergraduate enrollment FTE, (3) first-professional/graduate student

Table 6.2. Competing BBN Models with Different Threshold Values Specified

| | | | Prediction Accuracy (n = 21,662) | | |
Threshold	Number of Variables	Conditional Probability	Number of Correct Classification	Percentage	SD
6	21	52	20,734	95.72	0.27
8	16	35	19,946	92.08	0.36
10	13	20	19,155	88.43	0.43
12.5	11	13	18,029	83.23	0.50

Notes: Number of variables does not include the outcome variable (Carnegie classification). Numbers in the Threshold column are times of the system default value.

NEW DIRECTIONS FOR INSTITUTIONAL RESEARCH • DOI: 10.1002/ir

Figure 6.1. BBN Model of Carnegie Classification Based on NSOPF:99

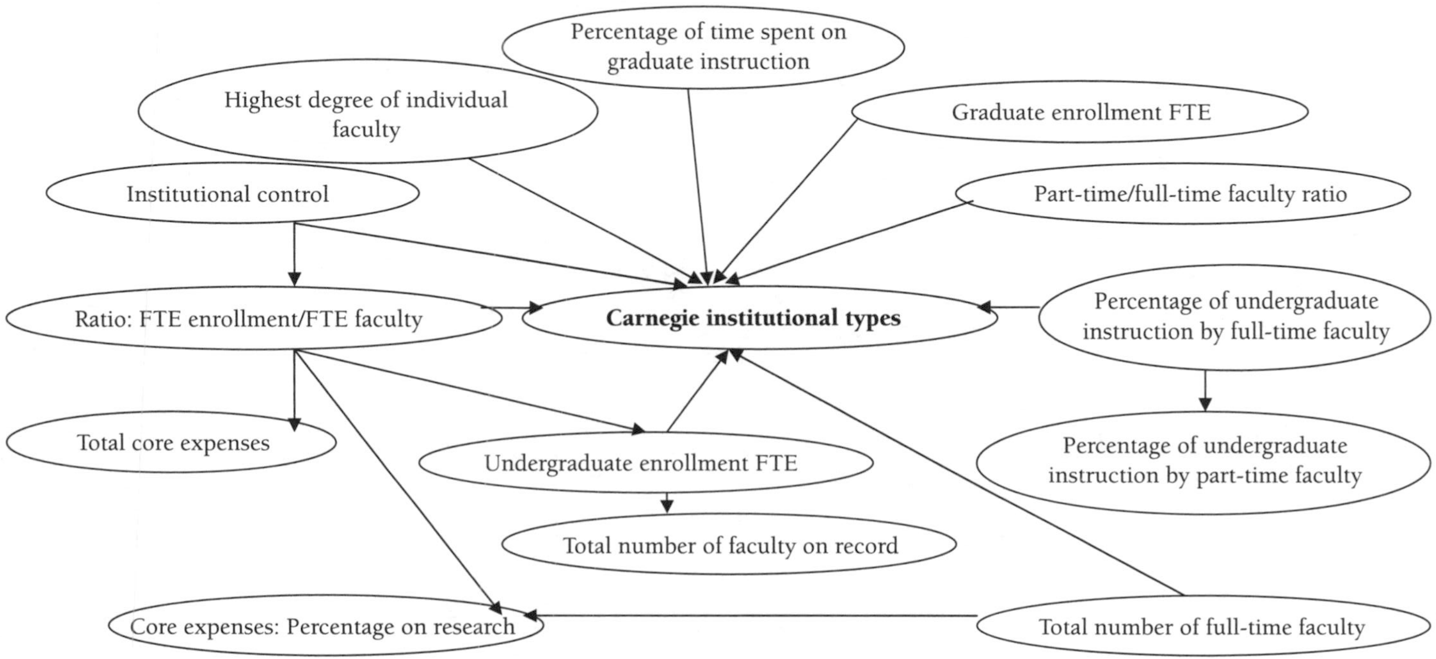

enrollment FTE, (4) percentage of undergraduate instruction by full-time faculty, (5) total number of full-time faculty, (6) ratio of part-time to full-time faculty members, (7) percentage of core expenses on research activities, (8) institutional control, (9) faculty member's highest degree, and (10) percentage of time spent on instruction of graduate/first-professional students. Except for the last two, all are institutional-level variables. In addition, three more institutional variables were found to have an indirect impact on faculty classification: total number of faculty on the institution list, percentage of undergraduate instruction by part-time faculty, and total institutional core expenses.

Along with the graphic model, a joint probability table is produced that has 4,520 entries and links the thirteen input variables to the output variable through probabilistic dependency. The table is too large to be presented here in its entirety, but a small fraction is shown in Table 6.3. There is one entry for each unique value combination of the thirteen input variables; the posterior probabilities (a faculty member predicted to be in any of the seven Carnegie institutional types) are calculated based on Bayes's rule and the highest probability indicates the most likely outcome category.

Presentation of the Findings.   According to the final BBN model, a few critical institutional characteristics explain how faculty members are categorized into certain Carnegie Classification types. Although the identified set of characteristics places individuals into the type of institutions according to the highest probability, some could have been classified into a different type of institution with a marginal difference in probabilities as shown with the example case of the third row in Table 6.3. Knowing that the faculty classification is mainly a function of institutional characteristics, institutions that have these marginal differences in probabilities may be interested in seeking what characteristics of their institutions led to the imprecise classifications or what they could do to move up the classification types. However, over forty-five hundred value combinations across thirteen input variables are too large to examine in detail when they are displayed in the joint probability table. It is particularly onerous to identify a unique combination of input variable values from such a large amount of combination sets.

One solution, to improve efficiency in using the results of BBN modeling, is to develop a user interface that searches the joint probability table and extracts the classification probability of any specific combination of institutional characteristics. Therefore, we developed an interactive program by using Microsoft Excel (2003) to implement this plan. Figure 6.2 shows the starting page of this program, where a user first selects the institutional control and faculty size on the left. After the OK button is pressed, another window comes up, and the user can specify more details of the institutional characteristics and click the Search Now button when ready. The program then displays the results of such selections in the probability (Figure 6.3). This small window in the middle of Figure 6.3 displays separate probabili-

Table 6.3. Conditional Probability of the BBN Model: Sample Entries

Case ID	Q17A1	X101Q0	Q32B	X10Q0	X13Q0	X35Q0	FACTOTAL	GradFTE
1	1	1	<0.5	<9.5	<1769	<30893	<294.5	<63
2	1	1	<0.5	<9.5	<1769	>102592,<399960	>804.5,<1645	>63,<2298
3	1	2	>30.5	>13.5,<17.5	>1769,<4294	>30893,<102592	>294.5,<804.5	>2298
4	2	1	>30.5	<9.5	<1769	<30893	>804.5,<1645	<63
5	2	2	<0.5	>9.5,<13.5	<1769	<30893	<294.5	<63
6	2	2	>0.5,<30.5	<9.5	<1769	>102592,<399960	>804.5,<1645	>63,<2298
7	2	2	>30.5	<9.5	<1769	<30893	<294.5	>63,<2298
8	2	2	>30.5	<9.5	<1769	>102592,<399960	>804.5,<1645	>63,<2298
9	2	2	>30.5	<9.5	<1769	<30893	<294.5	>63,<2298
10	3	1	<0.5	<9.5	<1769	>102592,<399960	>294.5,<804.5	>63,<2298
11	4	1	<0.5	>13.5,<17.5	>4294,<8768.5	>30893,<102592	>294.5,<804.5	>63,<2298
12	4	1	<0.5	>13.5,<17.5	>8768.5,<15840.5	>102592,<399960	>804.5,<1645	>63,<2298
13	4	1	<0.5	>17.5,<22.5	>15840.5	>102592,<399960	>804.5,<1645	>63,<2298
14	4	1	<0.5	>17.5,<22.5	>8768.5,<15840.5	>102592,<399960	>804.5,<1645	>63,<2298
15	4	1	>0.5,<30.5	>9.5,<13.5	<1769	<30893	<294.5	<63
16	4	1	>30.5	<9.5	<1769	>399960	>1645	>2298
17	4	1	>30.5	<9.5	>15840.5	>399960	>1645	>2298

Note: Because this table has too many columns to be presented on one page, it is divided into two parts. For each example case, the information continues in the second part of the table. Use the case ID as index. See Table 6.1 for variable information. Bold numbers indicate predicted outcome with highest probability.

(*continued*)

New Directions for Institutional Research • DOI: 10.1002/ir

Table 6.3. (continued)

Case ID	RESPCT	I1A	I19A	I19B	PTFTRT	Posterior Probabilities						
						1	2	3	4	5	6	7
1	<0.001	<135	<54.5	>40.5	>1.12	0.00	0.00	0.00	0.00	0.10	**0.87**	0.03
2	>0.070,<0.255	>361.5,<1147.5	>65.5,<80.5	>13.5,<23.5	<0.39	0.00	0.02	**0.98**	0.00	0.00	0.00	0.00
3	<0.001	>135,<361.5	<54.5	>40.5	>1.12	0.00	0.48	0.00	0.52	0.00	0.00	0.00
4	<0.001	<135	>65.5,<80.5	>23.5,<40.5	>1.12	0.00	0.00	0.00	0.00	0.10	0.15	**0.75**
5	<0.001	<135	>80.5	<13.5	>0.39,<1.12	0.00	0.00	0.00	0.00	**0.94**	0.00	0.06
6	>0.070,<0.255	>361.5,<1147.5	>65.5,<80.5	>23.5,<40.5	<0.39	0.00	0.41	**0.59**	0.00	0.00	0.00	0.00
7	<0.0001	<135	>54.5,<65.5	>40.5	>1.12	0.00	0.00	0.00	**0.89**	0.00	0.00	0.11
8	>0.255	>1147.5	<54.5	<13.5	<0.39	0.00	0.00	**1.00**	0.00	0.00	0.00	0.00
9	<0.001	<135	>54.5,<65.5	>23.5,<40.5	>0.39,<1.12	0.00	0.10	0.02	**0.67**	0.04	0.00	0.17
10	>0.001,<0.070	>361.5,<1147.5	>80.5	<13.5	<0.39	0.00	0.00	**1.00**	0.00	0.00	0.00	0.00
11	>0.001,<0.070	>135,<361.5	>65.5,<80.5	>13.5,<23.5	>0.39,<1.12	0.00	0.04	0.00	**0.94**	0.00	0.00	0.02
12	>0.255	>361.5,<1147.5	<54.5	>40.5	>0.39,<1.12	**0.67**	0.33	0.00	0.00	0.00	0.00	0.00
13	>0.001,<0.070	>361.5,<1147.5	>80.5	<13.5	<0.39	0.04	0.23	0.00	**0.73**	0.00	0.00	0.00
14	>0.001<0.070	>361.5,<1147.5	>80.5	<13.5	<0.39	0.01	0.08	0.00	**0.91**	0.00	0.00	0.00
15	<0.010	<135	>65.5,<80.5	>13.5,<23.5	>0.39,<1.12	0.00	0.00	0.00	0.01	0.38	0.10	**0.51**
16	>0.255	>1147.5	<54.5	<13.5	<0.39	0.00	**1.00**	0.00	0.00	0.00	0.00	0.00
17	>0.070,<0.255	>1147.5	>54.5,<65.5	>23.5,<40.5	>0.39,<1.12	**0.88**	0.12	0.00	0.00	0.00	0.00	0.00

Figure 6.2. BBN Interactive Program: Input Page

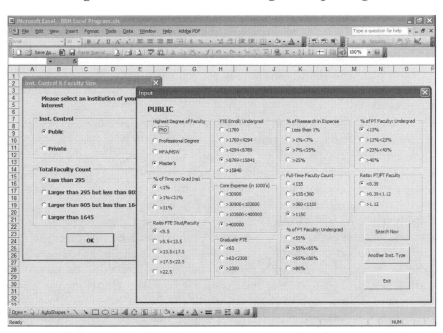

Figure 6.3. BBN Interactive Program: Outcome Page

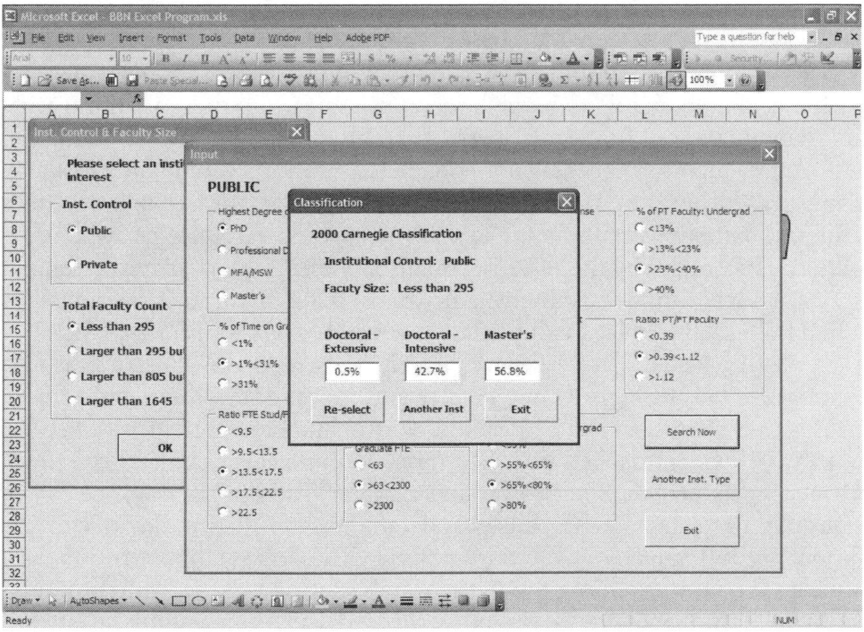

ties of the input case being classified into each of three Carnegie institutional categories.

The Microsoft Excel program is a communication tool for presenting the BBN findings in an easy and straightforward format to stakeholders. After receiving feedback from stakeholders, one can go back to the value selection page and modify the values of the institutional characteristics to examine how these values changes affect the classification probabilities in real time.

Interactive programs such as the one we illustrated here can be developed with the help of programming manuals widely available, such as *Microsoft Excel 2002 Visual Basic for Applications Step by Step* (Jacobson, 2001). In our interactive program, we wrote programming codes to modify one of the default Excel functions (Pivot Table) to run our queries of designated value combinations.

Bivariate Associations. What if the stakeholders ask the institutional researchers to explain how variables are related and how changes in one variable affect other variables? This is a weakness of BBN analysis: BBN models express relationships between variables through conditional probabilities, but probabilistic dependencies are of little use when we try to understand the strength of the relationships between variables. If needed, some statistical procedures can be used to get more detailed information about variable relationships. For instance, we calculated bivariate association or correlation for every pair of variables in the BBN model (Table 6.4). Pearson contingency coefficients (C) or biserial correlations are used because all variables are treated as nominal in BBN analysis. Depending on the original measurement scale of the variables, Pearson correlation or Spearman rho is also provided when appropriate.

Based on the output of the BBN model in this study, Carnegie classification is characterized as being largely influenced by the four input variables: graduate and first professional student enrollment FTE, the number of full-time faculty, percentage of core expenses on research, and total core expenses. Although one may argue that association measures sometimes underestimate the strength of relationship between variables because nominal measures convey the least information among the four measurement scales, association measures give a better estimate of variable relationships when the variable relationships depart severely from simple linearity. For example, the Pearson correlation between the percentage of undergraduate instruction taught by full-time faculty and the undergraduate enrollment FTE is only −0.02, but their Pearson contingency coefficient is 0.36 after both variables are binned into category-like intervals. A few of the input variables also have moderate bivariate relationships between themselves (for example, the total core expenses and number of full-time faculty or the number of full-time faculty and total number of faculty on institution list). Strong correlations among predictor variables might cause multicollinearity in linear multiple regression, but in BBN, correlations among input vari-

Table 6.4. Statistical Measures of Variable Association and Correlation

Variables	1	2	3	4	5	6	7	8	9	10	11	12	13
1 Core expenses, percentage on research	—												
2 Core expenses, total (in 1000's)	0.68 -0.74	—											
3 Enrollment FTE, undergraduate	**0.47** **-0.44**	**0.66** **-0.61**	—										
4 Enrollment FTE, graduate and first professional	0.63 -0.65	0.65 -0.89	0.55 -0.69	—									
5 Ratio of FTE enrollment/FTE faculty	**0.44** (-.39)	**0.45** (-.32)	**0.37** -0.11	**0.34** (-.24)	—								
6 Number faculty on institution list	0.6 -0.65	0.76 -0.79	0.68 -0.63	0.63 -0.8	**0.43** (-.30)	—							
7 Number of full-time faculty, fall 2003	0.67 -0.76	0.81 -0.9	0.67 -0.71	0.66 -0.88	**0.44** (-.33)	0.77 -0.91	—						
8 Undergraduate instruction: percentage part-time faculty	**0.26** -0.01	**0.26** (-.06)	**0.36** (-.02)	**0.28** (-.07)	**0.26** -0.05	**0.31** (-.10)	**0.27** 0	—					
9 Undergraduate instruction: percentage part-time faculty	**0.41** (-.37)	**0.34** (-.30)	**0.3** (-.15)	**0.37** (-.23)	**0.35** -0.2	**0.25** (-.16)	**0.35** (-.32)	0.64 (-.25)	—				
10 Ratio of part-time to full-time	**0.56** (-.26)	**0.47** (-.20)	**0.29** (-.15)	**0.47** (-.16)	**0.34** -0.04	**0.35** (-.13)	**0.5** (-.24)	**0.42** (-.26)	**0.6** -0.32	—			
11 Percentage time spent on instruction, graduate/first professional	**0.48** -0.24	**0.45** -0.21	**0.23** -0.11	**0.55** -0.28	-0.14 (-.16)	**0.39** -0.2	**0.46** -0.22	0.01 -0.11	-0.28 (-.14)	-0.37 -0.01	—		
12 Faculty member's highest degree	**0.39** [.36]	**0.34** [.30]	**0.2** [.14]	**0.4** [.38]	**0.29** [-.13]	**0.27** [.19]	**0.35** [.30]	**0.16** [.14]	**0.29** [-.25]	**0.39** [-.39]	0.35 [.34]	—	
13 Institution control, public versus private	.12	.20	.50	.02	.23	.28	.24	.14	.09	.01	.02	.10	—
14 2000 Carnegie code, 7 category	.70	.71	.67	.76	.52	.68	.72	.42	.49	.60	.51	0.51	.47

Note: Numbers in parentheses are Pearson correlations; numbers in brackets are Spearman rho. Other numbers are bivariate associations measured as Pearson contingency coefficients, biserial correlations, or phi. Bold numbers indicate the variable association stronger than their linear correlation.

NEW DIRECTIONS FOR INSTITUTIONAL RESEARCH • DOI: 10.1002/ir

ables can be used to fine tune the joint probabilities, and thereby improve model accuracy.

Probability Tables. Bivariate conditional probability tables can be made available to clarify variable relationships as well. While the variable association measures exhibit the strength of the relationship, probability tables assist researchers in determining the direction of the relationship. For example, conditional probabilities found in Table 6.5 (produced in SPSS) are useful in discussing the dependency between percentage undergraduate instruction by full-time faculty members and the Carnegie classification. These conditional probabilities indicate that if an institution has full-time faculty responsible for less than 55 percent of the undergraduate instruction, this institution is most likely in the Associate category ($p = .388$). If full-time faculty teach 55 to 65 percent undergraduate classes, the institution is most likely Doctoral-extensive ($p = .410$). If 66 to 79 percent undergraduate instruction is by full-time faculty, then the institution has the strongest likelihood to be Doctoral-extensive ($p = .383$). If more than 80 percent of the undergraduate instruction is the responsibility of full-time faculty, the institution is more likely to be Master's ($p = .350$) than other types. The four intervals of percentage undergraduate instruction by full-time faculty are defined to approximate uniform distribution.

Discussion

BBN has great potential in institutional research given the increasing popularity of large databases in postsecondary institutions. However, institutional researchers must be mindful of the drawbacks of this Bayesian data analysis approach. First, BBN analysis is often conducted in a black box manner, in which users rely on the algorithms embedded in the software for a final model. With an emphasis on model classification accuracy, the BBN analysis makes little information available on variable selection and other intermediate process of model construction. In spite of its efficiency, the automated variable selection in the black box operation deprives researchers of any detailed knowledge of the variable relationships except for what is presented in the final model. Thus, if the researchers need to gather more information about the data structure, such as the strength of variable relationships and their relative importance, BBN is not sufficient for the task, and complementary statistical techniques such as bivariate correlations and conditional probability tables may be needed.

Second, although the robustness and flexibility of BBN are enhanced through converting continuous variables into category-like measures, such variable transformation may involve information loss and reduce classification accuracy. Third, researchers need to be cautious about inferring causality based on the direction of variable dependency in the BBN model. Although Bayesian statisticians have confidence in the probabilistic modeling of causal relationships (Heckerman, 1997), the exploratory nature of BBN determines

Table 6.5. Sample Conditional Probability Table

Percentage Undergraduate Instruction by Full-Time Faculty	Doctoral-Extensive	Doctoral-Intensive	Medical	Master's	Baccalaureate	Associate	Other	Total
0 to 54 percent	0.157	0.079	0.063	0.184	0.072	**0.388**	0.058	1.0
55 to 65 percent	**0.410**	0.070	0.017	0.126	0.024	0.349	0.003	1.0
66 to 79 percent	**0.383**	0.132	0.013	0.250	0.035	0.166	0.021	1.0
80 to 100 percent	0.212	0.093	0.025	**0.350**	0.158	0.098	0.063	1.0

Note: Bold numbers indicate predicted outcome with highest probability.

that the identified relationships should be taken only as tentative hypotheses and potential directions for future research. If possible, findings in BBN should be validated with designed studies and expert judgments.

Finally, the data-driven nature of exploratory BBN analysis may cause researchers trained in classical statistics to doubt its validity in higher education studies. Indeed, Bayesian statistics started gaining momentum in the past decade as powerful algorithms in data mining, an analytical process designed to explore large amounts of data for consistent patterns or systematic relationships between variables. When initially introduced as a new discipline at the intersection of statistics, database management, machine learning and artificial intelligence, and computer science, data mining has been associated with "fishing" or "data snooping" (Hand, Mannila, and Smyth, 2001). Such skeptics' perceptions have been gradually changing with the recognition of the power of data mining in pattern visualization and exploratory analysis of massive data sets. Data mining techniques have been applied to higher education settings and have been discussed extensively in the New Directions for Institutional Research series (Luan and Zhao, 2006; Serban and Luan, 2002).

In our example, the BBN is empirical, meaning all probabilities are physically learned from data. We want to reiterate that BBN is a type of probability model with a unique feature: it permits the introduction of subjective prior knowledge into the probability calculations and the model building (Heckerman, 1997). Subjective prior knowledge, such as domain experts' beliefs about the dependencies among some variables, may be included in a BBN as prior probabilities and joined by evidence from objective data to propagate consistently through the network to have an impact on the probabilities of sequential outcomes. The adaptation of prior beliefs is a key element that differentiates Bayesian inferences from inferential models in classical non-Bayesian statistics. Some suggest that when subjective information is taken into consideration, a BBN can be only as useful as the prior knowledge is reliable, but it has also been verified that the effect of the prior probabilities diminishes as the sample size increases (Western, 1999).

Conclusion

In this chapter, we introduced BBN as a classification technique that works with large data sets and different types of variables. Using multinomial probabilistic inferences, BBN is robust against outliers, irregular distributions, and nonlinear variable relationships, and it is a powerful tool for exploratory analysis. Heckerman (1999) theorizes that a "Bayesian network can be viewed as a collection of probabilistic classification/regression models, organized by conditional-independence relationships" (p. 93). Computationally a BBN provides probabilistic inferences for an outcome variable through a network of input variables chained together by joint probabilities; any changes to a branch such as adding or removing variables would result in iterative updates and revision of the entire network. The enormous computational task explains why Bayesian models were not realized until powerful computers became available. If interested, readers are encouraged to study different algorithms that have been developed for learning and refining BBN, such as the exact Bayesian inferences with multivariate-normal distribution, approximation of missing data, selective model averaging, and learning and validating of causal relationships between variables (Heckerman, 1997, 1999).

The flexibility and robustness of BBN make it a useful tool for exploratory studies in institutional research. Examples of BBN applications include an investigation of factors influencing the college plans of high school students (Heckerman, 1997) and a prediction of student performance (Bekele and Menzel, 2005). Our example shows that BBN may also be used to investigate college ranking systems. Coupled with an interactive program, institutional researchers can instantaneously illustrate to institutional stakeholders how changes in parameters may improve or demote their institutions in ranking. However, like any other statistical procedure, BBN is merely another analytical technique that has strengths and limitations. Researchers should be fully informed how it functions and make applications in accordance with the problem under consideration.

As a final note, Bayesian statistics can be either parametric or nonparametric. BBN is only one type of application of Bayesian probability in nonparametric data analysis. Many other forms of Bayesian analysis have made early headway into scientific applications and educational research. For instance, Bayesian-based hierarchical modeling, Bayes factors for model selection or model averaging, Bayesian simulation methods for estimation, and Bayesian models for information retrieval have gained popularity (Blei, Jordan, and Ng, 2003; Western, 1999). This growing interest is primarily driven by the capacity of Bayesian statistics to account for rich sources of uncertainty in the context of empirical problems. With declining computing costs and increasing computational power, further advancement and broad use of Bayesian statistics are expected in all areas of academic research and real-life applications.

References

Bekele, R., and Menzel, W. "A Bayesian Approach to Predict Performance of a Student (BAPPS): A Case with Ethiopian Students." In M. Hamza (ed.), *Proceedings of Artificial Intelligence and Applications 2005*. Canada: ACTA Press, 2005.

Blei, D., Jordan, M., and Ng, A. "Hierarchal Bayesian Models for Applications in Information Retrieval." In J. Bernardo and others (eds.), *Bayesian Statistics 7: Proceedings of the Seventh Valencia International Meeting*. New York: Oxford University Press, 2003.

Cheng, J., and Greiner, R. "Comparing Bayesian Network Classifiers." In K. Laskey and H. Prade (eds.), *Proceedings of the Fifteenth Conference on Uncertainty in Artificial Intelligence*. San Francisco: Morgan Kaufmann, 1999.

Cheng, J., and others. "Learning Bayesian Networks from Data: An Information-Theory Based Approach." *Artificially Intelligence*, 2001, 137(1–2), 43–100.

Cumming, M. *Bayesian Belief Networks*. Retrieved March 20, 2003, from http://murrayc.com/learning/AI/bbn.shtml#Introduction.

Elder, J., and Pregibon, D. "A Statistical Perspective on Knowledge Discovery in Data-bases." In U. Fayyad, G. Piatetsky-Shapiro, R. Smyth, and R. Uthurusamy (eds.), *Advances in Knowledge Discovery and Data Mining.* Menlo Park, Calif.: AAAI/MIT Press, 1996.

Ferren, A., and Aylesworth, M. "Using Qualitative and Quantitative Information in Academic Decision Making." In R. Howard and K. Borland Jr. (eds.), *Balancing Qualitative and Quantitative Information for Effective Decision Support.* New Directions for Institutional Research, no. 112. San Francisco: Jossey-Bass, 2001.

Gillies, D. "Bayesianism and the Fixity of the Theoretical Framework." In D. Corfield and J. Williamson (eds.), *Foundations of Bayesianism.* Dordrecht: Kluwer Academic, 2001.

Hall, R. *Organizations: Structures, Processes, and Outcomes.* (4th ed.) Upper Saddle River, N.J.: Prentice Hall, 1995.

Hand, D. "Data Mining: Statistics and More?" *American Statistician,* 1998, 52, 112–118.

Hand, D. "Statistics and Data Mining: Intersecting Disciplines." *SIGKDD Exploration,* 1999, 1, 16–19.

Hand, D., Mannila, H., and Smyth, P. *Principles of Data Mining.* Cambridge, Mass.: MIT Press, 2001.

Heckerman, D. "Bayesian Networks for Data Mining." *Data Mining and Knowledge Discover,* 1997, 1, 79–119.

Heckerman, D. "A Tutorial on Learning with Bayesian Networks." In M. Jordan (Ed.), *Learning in Graphical Models.* Cambridge, Mass.: MIT Press, 1999.

Jacobson, R. *Microsoft Excel 2002: Visual Basic for Applications Step by Step.* Seattle, Wash.: Microsoft Press, 2001.

Luan, J. "Data Mining and Its Applications in Higher Education." In A. Serban and J. Luan (eds.), *Knowledge Management: Building a Competitive Advantage in Higher Education.* New Directions for Institutional Research, no. 113. San Francisco: Jossey-Bass, 2002.

Luan, J., and Zhao, C. (eds.). *Data Mining in Action: Case Studies of Enrollment Management.* New Directions for Institutional Research, no. 131. San Francisco: Jossey-Bass, 2006.

Niedermayer, D. *An Introduction to Bayesian Networks and Their Contemporary Applications.* 1998. Retrieved Sept. 24, 2003, from http://www.niedermayer.ca/ papers/ bayesian/.

Pearl, J. "Causal Diagrams for Empirical Research." *Biometrika,* 1995, 82, 669–710.

Pednault, E. "Statistical Learning Theory." In R. Wilson and F. Keil (eds.) *MIT Encyclopedia of the Cognitive Sciences.* Cambridge, Mass.: MIT Press, 1999.

Serban, A., and Luan, J. (eds.). *Knowledge Management: Building a Competitive Advantage in Higher Education.* New Directions for Institutional Research, no. 113. San Francisco: Jossey-Bass, 2002.

Singh, M., and Provan, G. "A Comparison of Induction Algorithms for Selective and Non-Selective Bayesian Classifiers." In A. Prieditis and S. Russell (eds.), *Proceedings of the Twelfth International Conference on Machine Learning.* San Francisco: Morgan Kaufmann, 1995.

Western, B. "Bayesian Analysis for Sociologists: An Introduction." *Sociological Methods and Research,* 1999, 28(1), 7–34.

Winkler, R. *An Introduction to Bayesian Inference and Decision.* New York: Holt, 1972.

YONGHONG JADE XU *is an assistant professor in the educational research program at the University of Memphis.*

TERRY T. ISHITANI *is an assistant professor in the educational research program at the University of Memphis.*

Many existing studies have failed to address issues related to the timing of student departure from college. This chapter proposes event history modeling to assess when students depart.

How to Explore Timing of Intervention for Students at Risk of Departure

Terry T. Ishitani

Student departure from postsecondary institutions has been one of the central topics of concern discussed widely by policymakers, institutional personnel, and educational researchers at various levels. For instance, at the national level, 32 percent of those who entered in the postsecondary system between 1995 and 1996 left their institutions within three years (Bradburn, 2003). Some may consider that this attrition rate is still high, particularly given that the rate of entry into four-year institutions for the United States is lower than the average of twenty-six other countries (National Center for Education Statistics, 2004). (The U.S. entry rate for four-year institutions was 42 percent in 2001; Finland, New Zealand, Norway, and Sweden had entry rates of over 60 percent.) At the institutional level, the persistence rate is the most commonly used indicator for institutional performance and is frequently subject to intense scrutiny by stakeholders. Persistence rates become much more salient for institutions when their operational budgets largely depend on the income generated by student tuition and fees. For such institutions, higher attrition rates directly lead to reduction in funding. Furthermore, the importance of this topic is clearly signified not only in voluminous numbers of scholastic publications on college attrition, but also in the *Journal of College Student Retention*, which focuses solely on issues surrounding college student departure.

In the area of educational research, researchers have developed numerous models and theories to understand the roots of college attrition (Bean,

New Directions for Institutional Research, no. 137, Spring 2008 © Wiley Periodicals, Inc.
Published online in Wiley InterScience (www.interscience.wiley.com) • DOI: 10.1002/ir.241

1980; Cabrera, Castaneda, Nora, and Hengstler, 1992; Chickering and Reisser, 1993; Metzner and Bean, 1987; Pascarella, 1980; Tinto, 1975). Braxton (2000) offered a classification for different theoretical frameworks of college retention based on their orientations (such as economic, organizational, psychological, and sociological perspectives). Among all the existing retention theories, Tinto's student-to-environment interactive retention theory (1975) has been among the most widely used in the literature. Tinto argues that positive ongoing academic and social experiences on campus improve student persistence. Many recognize the importance of students' involvement in academic and social communities and its relation to student persistence, which prompted numerous attrition studies evolving around Tinto's theoretical framework.

In addition to the educational research community, perspectives derived from various college attrition theories are reflected in the development of programs or curricula designed to strengthen student persistence on campus. One example is learning communities, which allow groups of students to take linked courses: "one of a variety of curricular structures that link together several existing courses—or actually restructure the curricular material entirely—so that students have opportunities for deeper understanding of and integration of the material they are learning, and more interaction with one another and their teachers . . ." (Gabelnick, MacGregor, Matthews, and Smith, 1990, p. 19). Curriculum programs such as learning communities focus on having students more involved academically and socially. Particularly for freshman students whose attachment to the institution is still tenuous, this type of program has been found to be effective in improving academic performance and retention (Soldner, Lee, and Duby, 1999). Although academic and social integration clearly matters most during the first year of college, given that student departure occurs at any point during enrollment, should we rest assured that students will finish college once they are involved in a program such as learning communities? Tinto (2002) emphasizes the importance of advice and support for college success. Is there any model for institutional personnel, such as academic advisors and faculty, to monitor the departure risks of their students over time, which can be also used as a tool to communicate with various units on campus for the purpose of reducing such risks?

This chapter discusses the longitudinal nature of college attrition and introduces a statistical technique suited for assessing longitudinal student departure behavior. In addition, examples of simulation models that are designed to graphically illustrate student departure risks are presented.

Time Dimension in Student Departure

The attrition and retention models offered by Tinto (1975) and Bean (1980) are perhaps the most widely recognized theoretical frameworks for college persistence behavior. Both models view retention longitudinally and emphasize interactions between students and institutional environments (see Figure 7.1 for Tinto's integration model). The models by Tinto and Bean have

Figure 7.1. Tinto's Integration Model

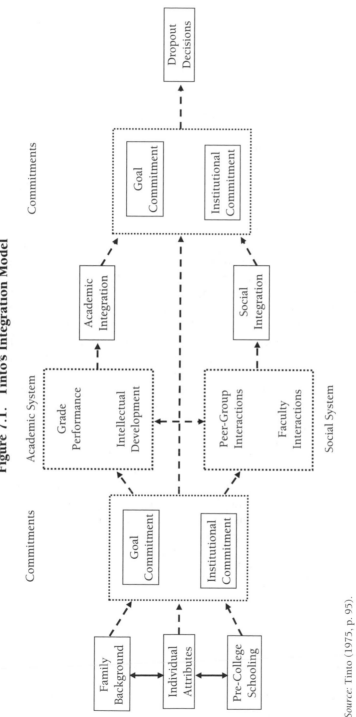

Source: Tinto (1975, p. 95).

been widely applied in research studies that have helped advance under-standing of college attrition in our educational system. Carbrera, Nora, and Castaneda (1993) further proposed their conversion model between the models developed by Tinto and Bean. They suggested that these two mod-els were not necessarily mutually exclusive, even given that the models were based on different theoretical orientations. Findings using these two mod-els were rather complementary to each other. Thus, one can address the issue of student departure more comprehensively when these two models are merged into one model. Some of recent studies using Tinto's theoretical perspectives focused more on effects of certain model components on depar-ture. Braxton, Milem, and Sullivan (2000) found that active learning signif-icantly influenced social integration, which led to a decision to stay at the institutions. Another study by Liu and Liu (2000) ascertained the impor-tance of academic integration and student satisfaction to college persistence.

The theoretical attrition and retention models developed by Tinto and Bean have been successful in elucidating how student departure occurs in reference to the causal relations. However, many studies that attempted to faithfully replicate Tinto's model often failed to incorporate the departure timing in their research. Thus, they overlook how dimensions of time affect student departure behavior. In Figure 7.1 the final outcome in Tinto's model is specified as "dropout decisions," which is a result of students' experiencing various components in a sequence. In existing attrition stud-ies, this outcome variable is often defined as aggregated enrollment status of students, which is usually either enrolled or not enrolled. However, this variable does not indicate when exactly students left the institution. It is logical to assume that the first-year departure may be different from the third-year departure in nature. For instance, students might have left the institution during the first year because of a lack of social support, whereas others might transfer to other institutions during the third year because they were not content with courses in their major programs. Thus, it is more appropriate to assess student departure behavior by some type of discrete time frame instead of using an aggregated enrollment status. More-over, in many studies, this aggregated dichotomous variable did not reveal what type of departure students experienced, such as dropout, academic dismissal, or transfer. As Metzner and Bean (1987) noted, finding results in attrition research can be spurious if taking different types of departure are not taken into account.

In reality, student persistence is a longitudinal process and is quite often discussed in the form of rates among researchers and policymakers, which are measured at discrete points in time, such as first-year and second-year persistence rates. However, comparisons based on simple descriptive unad-justed persistence rates across different groups such as race are misleading, because effects of other observable variables, such as gender and academic aptitudes, are not taken into account for estimating these persistence rates (DesJardins, Ahlburg, and McCall, 2006). Therefore, adjusted rates that are produced using statistical procedures may be more valuable and informative for the educational policy purpose.

Figure 7.2 illustrates a longitudinal schema of student departure in which students enter a postsecondary institution with various precollege characteristics. Interactions between the students and institutional environment shape the quality of collegiate experiences for students. Such interactions include student involvement exemplified as academic and social integration specified in Tinto's model. However, academic and social integration are stipulated as events in Figure 7.1. Notice that variables such as student involvement are listed independently for each academic year, and their values and effects on enrollment decisions are assumed to vary across academic years in Figure 7.2. It is logical to assume that students develop their academic and social network at different rates and degrees. Thus, it is necessary to treat these variables as a longitudinal process instead of an event. In Figure 7.2, departure types are clearly separated instead of aggregated status. Student departure includes dropout, transfer, stop-out (noncontinuous enrollment), and academic dismissal.

Methodological Approach to Longitudinal Student Departure

Structural equation modeling has been a popular statistical technique in previous attrition and retention studies, in particular when researchers attempted to faithfully replicate Tinto's model. When this approach is used, research results are typically explained as how well the study sample fits Tinto's retention schema and to what degree explanatory variables affect a departure decision. Although validating how robust certain retention theories are for different types of students or institutions is an important issue in advancing understanding of student departure behavior, institutional decision makers or personnel may find it less useful to improve efficiency in their educational practice. They may be more interested in gathering information on first-year programs that are effective in improving the first-year retention rate. In addition to these programs, what makes their practice more efficient is to know which students are more likely to leave and in what period of time. By knowing departure risk profiles of students and the timing of student departure, institutional personnel such as advisors and faculty can calibrate the intensity of their intervention to prevent students at risk of departure from leaving the institution, which has a direct impact on the institutional persistence rate.

There are several feasible statistical approaches that allow us to explore student departure in a manner illustrated in Figure 7.2. Event history modeling, also known as survival analysis, is well suited for this type of investigation. This statistical technique has a number of advantages for college attrition research. First, it analyzes a dichotomous variable such as enrolled or not enrolled more appropriately than linear regression techniques do. Second, it offers results translated in the form of departure probability, that

Figure 7.2. Longitudinal College Persistence Schema

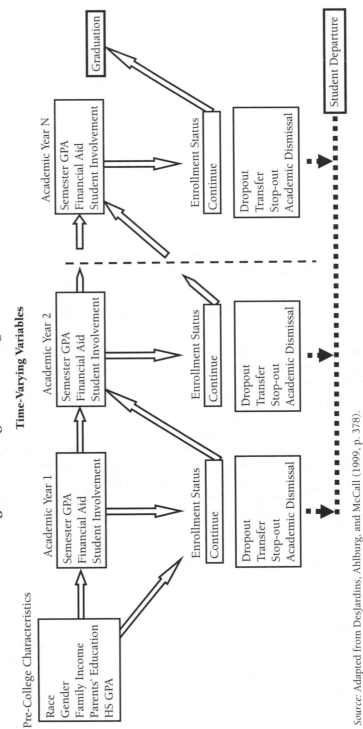

Time-Varying Variables

Pre-College Characteristics

Race
Gender
Family Income
Parents' Education
HS GPA

Academic Year 1

Semester GPA
Financial Aid
Student Involvement

Academic Year 2

Semester GPA
Financial Aid
Student Involvement

Academic Year N

Semester GPA
Financial Aid
Student Involvement

Graduation

Enrollment Status

Continue

Enrollment Status

Continue

Enrollment Status

Continue

Dropout
Transfer
Stop-out
Academic Dismissal

Dropout
Transfer
Stop-out
Academic Dismissal

Dropout
Transfer
Stop-out
Academic Dismissal

Student Departure

Source: Adapted from DesJardins, Ahlburg, and McCall (1999, p. 378).

is, how variables contribute to increasing or decreasing the chance of dropout in percentage instead of how large or small variables affect dropout in the structural equation modeling. Third, it analyzes departure behaviors that are unique to specific time periods, such as first-year or first-semester dropout. Fourth, it estimates effects of variables such as semester grade point averages (GPAs) that change values over time on student departure. Finally, it allows researchers to select different types of departure, such as dropout, academic dismissal, and transfer, without creating a separate data set for each type of departure.

A handful of studies have applied event history modeling to examine issues on college student persistence (DesJardins, Ahlburg, and McCall, 1999; Murtaugh, Burns, and Schuster, 1999; Ishitani, 2003, 2006; Ishitani and DesJardins, 2002). This modeling technique can be a powerful tool, particularly when the researcher is interested in comparing persistence behavior between a special interest group of students and their counterparts. Instead of comparing percentage differences in leavers between the two groups, assessing departure behaviors between these groups reveals more information when event history modeling is used. For instance, I examined college attrition of first-generation students using event history modeling and institutional data (Ishitani, 2003).

This study sample included a cohort of 1,747 freshman students and their used enrollment status for each semester over a period of five academic years. About 58 percent of the sample were first-generation students. Twenty-six percent of the initial cohort were students with one college-educated parent, and 16 percent had two college-educated parents. Departure was defined in the study as a student's first spell of departure from the study institution and included different types of departure, such as dropouts, transfers, academic dismissals, and stop-outs (in other words, some departed students may return and resume their enrollment after a certain period of discontinuation). Table 7.1 presents percentages of enrolled students at the end of each semester by parents' educational attainment over

Table 7.1. Percentage of Enrolled Students by Parents' Educational Attainment

Semester	First Generation	One College-Educated Parent	Both Parents College Educated
1	0.833	0.898	0.913
2	0.635	0.698	0.714
3	0.552	0.621	0.657
4	0.491	0.555	0.614
5	0.423	0.537	0.584
6	0.426	0.501	0.541

Source: Adapted from Ishitani (2003, p. 442).

the first six semesters. At the end of the first semester, approximately 17 percent of first-generation students left the study institution, and 9 percent of students with both college-educated parents did. The gap between the number of first-generation students and students with college-educated parents existed to the end of the six semesters.

Based on the descriptive statistics in Table 7.1, first-generation students appeared to have a higher departure rate than other students. However, a more interesting inquiry may be how being a first-generation student really affects one's departure behavior after controlling for other student characteristics, such as high school GPA. One of the modeling techniques within event history modeling is exponential modeling, a basic estimation model. In this modeling, estimates are assumed to increase or decrease exponentially over time depending on whether coefficients have positive or negative values. Table 7.2 shows results of departure estimates based on exponential modeling. Since maximum likelihood estimation is applied in event history modeling, one may use a formula, $\exp(\alpha) - 1$, where α represents a coefficient value to interpret impact of each explanatory variable (relative risk). For instance, the coefficient value for being a first-generation student in Table 7.2 is 0.253. Using the formula above, one obtains $\exp(0.253) - 1 = 0.288$. Given that departure was coded as 1 (enrolled = 0), this is interpreted as first-generation students being approximately 29 percent more likely to depart in the first year than students with college-educated parents.

However, by applying the exponential model in studies of student attrition, researchers assume that the unit of risk is equidistant and the magnitude of this risk increases or decreases exponentially over time. As mentioned earlier, students may leave their institutions for different reasons

Table 7.2. Results from the Exponential Model

Variable	Label	Coefficient	Relative Risk	Significance
Constant		−0.600		*
Gender	Female	0.142	0.153	*
Race	Minority	−0.066	−0.064	
Parents' Education	First generation	0.253	0.288	*
	One parent with college degree	0.027	0.027	
Annual Family Income	$25,000 or less	0.209	0.232	*
	$25,000–$45,000	0.032	0.033	
Size of Hometown	Fewer than 5,000 residents	0.051	0.052	
	More than 50,000 residents	0.017	0.017	
High School GPA	Continuous	−0.650	−0.478	*

$*p < 0.05$.

Source: Adapted from Ishitani (2003, p. 443).

at different times. Thus, I considered that the assumption for this model as departure risk increasing exponentially did not fit the nature of college student attrition. In order to improve fit between event history modeling and the nature of student departure behavior, the period-specific piecewise hazard model was selected to investigate departure behavior in the data. This approach estimates conditional departure risks at discrete points in time.

Table 7.3 shows the results estimated by period-specific piecewise hazard modeling. Coefficient estimates for each year were conditional, that is, for instance, coefficients for the second year were estimated based on a group of students who completed the first year (without students who departed during the first year). Coefficients for being a first-generation student fluctuated over time in Table 7.3. First-generation students faced the highest risk of departure during their first year. They were 71 percent more likely to leave the study institution than students with college-educated parents. This estimated first-year departure risk using the period-specific piecewise hazard model was much higher than the 29 percent estimated by the exponential model. Thus, one may underestimate the departure risk for first-generation students in their first year using the exponential model. Furthermore, one can observe that subsequent departure risks for first-generation students did not increase as assumed in exponential modeling. The risk of departure decreased for the second year (15 percent), but first-generation students again faced a higher risk of departure in the third year (60 percent) after completing their second year. Institutional personnel are empirically aware of higher attrition rates during the first year of college, which have resulted in efforts in developing intervention programs to reduce the departure rate. However, based on study findings here, such efforts should be extended to the third year. Disclosure of such longitudinal profiles of student departure is extremely difficult to attain by using a conventional statistical technique to examine student departure behavior.

Furthermore, when explanatory variables such as gender and race are held constant, event history modeling allows one to examine if their effects are also constant over time. In addition, event history techniques allow researchers to control for variables that change in value over time, such as semester GPAs. In Table 7.3, effects of semester GPAs are displayed under time-varying effect. Inclusion of such a time-varying variable was designed to enhance coefficient estimates for other explanatory variables.

Illustration of longitudinal student departure behavior has significant and valuable implications for our educational practice. For instance, using the coefficient estimates in Table 7.3, consider students A and B, who have different student characteristics. Student A has low-risk characteristics of departure, and student B has high-risk characteristics of departure. Student A (B) is a male (female) student from a small town (a large town), has a family income of $46,000 ($23,000), and has two college-educated parents (first-generation student). Projected departure risks for both students are displayed in Figure 7.3. Student A, whose parents are both college educated, is expected to have his highest departure risk in the first year, and

Table 7.3. Results from Period-Specific Piecewise Hazard Model

Variable	Label	First Year			Second Year			Third Year			Fourth Year			Fifth Year		
		Coeff[a]	Relative Risk	Sig[b]	Coeff[a]	Relative Risk	Sig[b]	Coeff[a]	Relative Risk	Sig[b]	Coeff[a]	Relative Risk	Sig[b]	Coeff[a]	Relative Risk	Sig[b]
Constant		-2.387		*	-2.273		*	-2.768		*	-4.740		*	-2.361		*
Gender	Female	0.236	0.266		0.108	0.114		0.448	0.565	*	0.475	0.607	*	0.080	0.083	*
Race	Minority	-0.557	-0.427	*	-0.411	-0.337	*	-0.403	-0.332		0.228	0.256		-0.377	-0.314	
Parents' Education	First generation	0.534	0.705	*	0.138	0.148		0.473	0.604	*	-0.307	-0.264		0.227	0.225	
	One parent with college degree	0.050	0.051		0.171	0.187		0.250	0.284		-0.242	-0.215		0.257	0.293	
Annual Family Income	$25,000 or less	0.400	0.492	*	0.229	0.257	*	0.261	0.299		0.066	0.069		-0.076	-0.074	
	$25,000–$45,000	0.039	0.039		0.076	0.079		0.091	0.095		0.111	0.117		-0.061	-0.059	
Size of Hometown	Fewer than 5,000 residents	0.263	0.301		-0.061	-0.059		-0.251	-0.022		0.448	0.565		-0.102	-0.097	
	More than 50,000 residents	0.226	0.253		-0.223	-0.200	*	0.140	0.151		0.186	0.204		-0.303	-0.029	
High School GPA	Continuous	-0.554	-0.425	*	-0.076	-0.073		-0.318	-0.273		0.336	0.399		0.278	0.320	
Time-Varying Effect	College GPA less than 2.00	1.356	2.880	*	1.345	2.837	*	1.391	3.017	*	1.752	4.767	*	1.036	1.818	*

*$p < 0.05$.

[a]Coeff = coefficient.

[b]Sig = significance.

Source: Adapted from Ishitani (2003, p. 443).

Figure 7.3. Hypothesized Departure Risks for Students A and B

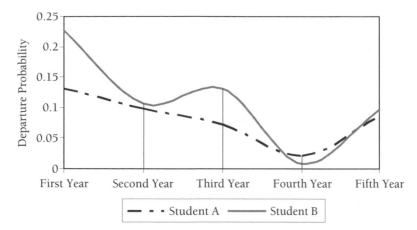

his departure wanes as he proceeds through college. Student B, a first-generation student in this instance, has a much higher risk of departure than student A in the first year. Although both students are expected to have similar departure risks during the second year, student B is assumed to have a higher risk of departure than student A in the third year. Such a graphic display of departure risks allows institutional personnel such as academic advisors and faculty to monitor students at risk of departure each academic year and intensify their interactions with such students before these students leave their institutions.

After controlling for factors such as financial aid and institutional selectivity, I investigated first-generation college students and their longitudinal persistence behavior using a national data set (2006). In this study, first-generation students faced the highest risk of departure during the second year of college. Based on the research findings from these two studies, first-generation students are more likely to depart at particular time periods than students whose mother and father are college educated.

In addition to examining college attrition among different types of students, some may be interested in applying event history modeling for different types of departure behaviors such as stop-out. Detrimental issues revolving around noncontinuous enrollment widely known as stop-out include prolonging time to graduation, higher total costs for higher education (given steady increases in tuitions and fees over time), and delaying entry into the workforce. Thus, negative outcomes of stop-out behavior have raised concerns among policymakers, and educational researchers are expected to investigate college stop-out behavior in detail. However, unlike examining a single occurrence of certain student departure types, many stop-out students repeat their discontinuation, that is, the number of episodes of noncontinuous enrollment varies among stop-outs. This feature unique to stop-out students makes model designing and interpretation of results challenging.

DesJardins, Ahlburg, and McCall (2006) presented their research findings on multiple episodes of college student stop-out behaviors using event history modeling. They particularly focused on the impact of ethnicity, academic ability (ACT composite scores), and family income on stop-out behavior after controlling for factors such as financial aid and age. They found that Asian Americans were least likely to stop out for the first time than African American, Caucasian, and Hispanic students and were more likely to return from their first stop-out episode. Interestingly, Asian Americans and African Americans had slightly higher stop-out rates for the second time than Caucasian and Hispanic students. As for how family income affects stop-out behavior, high-income students showed small advantages over low-income students. The probability that high-income students would experience stop-out was 66 percent; for low-income students, it was 73 percent. However, the chance that high-income students would return was 48 percent, while the probability that low-income students would return was 47 percent. Thus, the level of family income is associated with the possibility that students will discontinue their enrollment, but it has little effect on whether they will return. Studies such as that by DesJardins, Ahlburg, and McCall shed light on issues known as being rather complex in the research of college student departure.

Simulation Models Using Study Results

Advanced statistical techniques such as event history modeling, designed to assess the process of certain events, can be applied to existing educational issues and topics that have never been investigated in a longitudinal framework. Given the numerous advantages provided by this technique, we can expect to improve our understanding of these educational issues and topics. However, the parameters in event history modeling are estimated by maximum likelihood method. Unlike estimates obtained by conventional statistical techniques, some may find the parameters yielded by event history techniques somewhat baffling. Many researchers do not explain how to interpret these parameters in their studies. Furthermore, with some types of event history modeling such as period-specific hazard models, the outcome parameters are displayed in numerous columns in tables, and the extent of the information offered may make it difficult to grasp the study findings as a whole.

Although graphical display of longitudinal departure is a valuable aid in targeting at-risk students using Figure 7.3, the graphs in Figure 7.3 were created by computing risk probabilities manually. In order to assist institutional personnel and decision makers in gaining benefits from such studies using event history modeling, I often develop simulation model programs for my studies. Such programs are effective tools in educational practice or decision-making processes when the goal is to make complex study results easier to understand. It is ideal when one can view graphically displayed student departure risks instantaneously by inputting different values for explanatory variables. This is more dynamic and inspiring than analysis results displayed in the static form of tables. A simulation program that allows real-time parameter input also helps researchers respond quickly to options requested by stakeholders who may have diverse interests.

Figure 7.4 is an image of the input interface of the simulation program where one selects student characteristics of interest. The program was developed by Microsoft Visual Basic (Version 6.0). Unlike programs developed by other software such as Microsoft Excel, where users need this particular software to run programs, this simulation program is an .exe file and does not require any particular software to run the program. A series of variables appearing in the input interface were analyzed for their effects on student departure using event history modeling prior to development of this simulation model. Thus, parameter values estimated in the analysis were used to create the program. After inputting individual values for the parameters, the user can proceed to the next page, where probabilities of student departure and graduation are graphically displayed by pressing a command button, Estimate, on this input page.

Figure 7.5 is an image of the output generated by this program. The graph on the left illustrates departure probabilities by academic year. These

Figure 7.4. Image of Input Interface

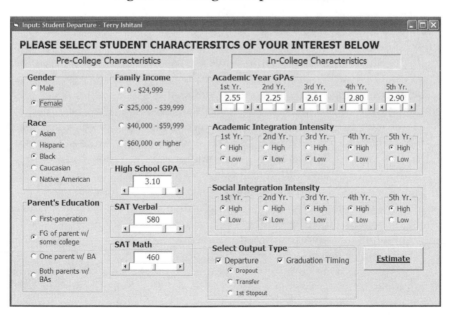

Figure 7.5. Image of Output Interface

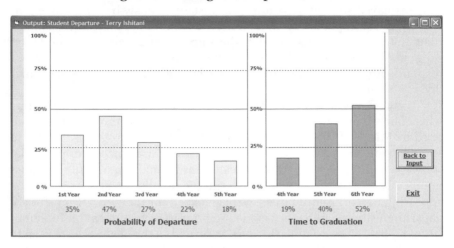

departure probabilities were estimated based on a subsample of students who successfully completed a previous academic year; students who departed were excluded from departure risk estimations for subsequent years. On the right, probabilities of graduation are presented by different timing of graduation. Timing of graduation was also estimated in the same manner as student departure, with students who graduated in the fourth year being excluded from estimation of the fifth year graduation probability.

After reviewing departure and graduation probabilities on the output interface, the user can go back to the input page by pressing Back to Input to apply altered parameter values. In the input interface, student characteristics on the left should remain the same, while the parameters on the right should be adjusted to learn if such adjustments reduce departure risks for different academic years. For instance, particular combinations of academic social integration may moderate spikes in departure risk for students with certain pre-college characteristics. Thus, knowing such combinations can guide academic advisors and faculty to advocate for these students with relevant activities or curricula programs such as learning communities on campus. Furthermore, given that students have different levels of departure risks at varying points in time, such departure risks graphically displayed in Figure 7.5 assist academic advisors and faculty members in improving efficiency in their educational practice by targeting students according to their timing of departure, and calibrating the intensity of their intervention with these students.

The simulation model exemplified above is designed to demonstrate the potential of using computer programming in the area of institutional research. Such simulation programs can be easily improved by adding additional interface pages or another set of characteristics for a second student.

For instance, the user may develop another interface that allows him or her to keep the record of student profiles for later review (for example, see Figure 7.6). Sharing student profiles that include predicted departure risks graphically displayed with other units on campus not only helps institutional personnel organize intervention plans for individual students more efficiently but also enriches campus networking.

Application of simulation models is not limited to illustrating longitudinal student attrition. Other programs can be designed and developed to stimulate discussion in the area of students' enrollment decision, optimizing institutional scholarship offers, and student recruitment strategies. (I can be contacted for more information on simulation models in these areas.) Institutional researchers may develop simulation models using data or information that they already have but relating them to student departure. For example, many institutions participate in the National Survey of Student Engagement (NSSE), and the institutional research office often oversees this project at many campuses. The NSSE survey is typically administered during the spring semester. In the following fall semester, institutional researchers identify the enrollment status of those who participated in the survey, which can be linked to the NSSE results. Figure 7.7 exemplifies a simulation model that assists in determining what type of engagement may be beneficial during a student's first-year of college to improve the chance that the student will return for the second year.

Finally, and most important, such simulation programs should be mainly developed as tools or references for decision making, not as devices

Figure 7.6. Image of Output Record

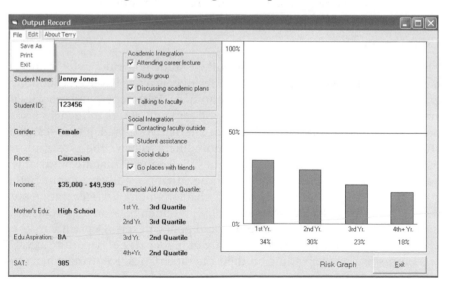

**Figure 7.7. Second-Year Return Simulation Model Based
on NSSE Results**

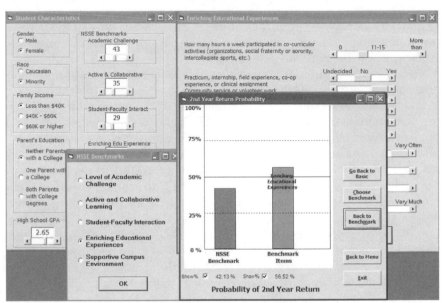

to project students' departure and their timing with precise accuracy or to
provide absolute solutions for academic endeavors of students. Such modeling programs are designed to stimulate one's thinking and offer more
dynamic and effective alternatives to use research results.

Conclusion

This chapter has discussed issues on college student attrition with timing of
departure being taken into account. College persistence has been commonly
examined using structural equation techniques. Researchers and scholars in
such studies mainly focus on how a wide array of factors influences a student's enrollment decision. I propose an alternative approach to investigate
student attrition: when students are more likely to leave their institutions
using event history modeling techniques. Selecting explanatory variables
based on empirical findings from previous attrition studies, I conducted a
study to assess longitudinal departure behavior among first-generation students. Departure risks that are graphically presented have an important util-
itarian value to institutional personnel and policymakers. Departure risks of
students vary over time, and students are at higher risk of departure at various points in time depending on their characteristics. Knowing when stu-

dents are more likely to leave assists institutional personnel in designing systematic intervention plans to lower the institutional attrition rate.

In spite of practical benefits from longitudinal student departure studies, findings from such studies are often rather difficult to interpret. In many cases, institutional personnel and policymakers are looking for concrete information to assist them in their educational practice and decision making, not study results expressed in mysterious numerical values. A solution to this dilemma is to develop interactive programs to deliver research results to stakeholders in a way that they can gain a better understanding of the issue of their interests. The examples in this chapter were developed using Visual Basic programming techniques. However, as you see in other chapters in this volume of New Directions for Institutional Research, other contributing authors have used other software or programs to attain similar effects. Presenting research results using computer programming allows researchers to respond to questions from decision makers instantaneously and stimulate lively discussion. Application of such simulation modeling has a great deal of promise in the area of institutional research and the educational research community in general.

References

Bean, J. "Dropouts and Turnover: The Synthesis and Test of a Causal Model of Student Attrition." *Research in Higher Education,* 1980, *12*(2), 155–187.

Bradburn, E. *Short-Term Enrollment in Postsecondary Education: Student Background and Institutional Differences in Reasons for Early Departure.* Washington, D.C.: National Center for Education Statistics, U.S. Department of Education, 2002.

Braxton, J. "Reinvigorating Theory and Research on the Departure Puzzle." In J. Braxton (ed.), *Reworking the Student Departure Puzzle.* Nashville, Tenn.: Vanderbilt University Press, 2000.

Braxton, J., Milem, J., and Sullivan, A. "The Influence of Active Learning on the College Student Departure Process: Toward a Revision of Tinto's Theory." *Journal of Higher Education,* 2000, *71*(5), 569–590.

Cabrera, A., Castaneda, M., Nora, A., and Hengstler, D. "The Convergence Between Two Theories of College Persistence." *Journal of Higher Education,* 1992, *63*(2), 143–164.

Chickering, A., and Reisser, L. *Education and Identity.* San Francisco: Jossey-Bass, 1993.

DesJardins, S., Ahlburg, A., and McCall, B. "An Event History Model of Student Departure." *Economics of Education Review,* 1999, *18*(3), 375–390.

DesJardins, S., Ahlburg, D., and McCall, B. "The Effects of Interrupted Enrollment on Graduation from College: Racial, Income, and Ability Differences." *Economics of Education Review,* 2006, *25*(6), 575–590.

Gabelnick, F., MacGregor, J., Matthews, R., and Smith, B. "Learning Community Models." In F. Gabelnick, J. MacGregor, R. Matthews, and B. Smith (eds.), *Learning Communities: Creating Connections among Students, Faculty, and Disciplines.* New Directions for Teaching and Learning, no. 41. San Francisco: Jossey-Bass, 1990.

Ishitani, T. "A Longitudinal Approach to Assessing Attrition Behavior Among First-generation Students: Time-Varying Effects of Pre-College Characteristics." *Research in Higher Education,* 2003, *44*(4), 433–449.

Ishitani, T. "Studying Attrition and Degree Completion Behavior Among First-generation College Students in the United States." *Journal of Higher Education,* 2006, *77*(5), 861–885.

Ishitani, T., and DesJardins, S. "A Longitudinal Investigation of Dropout from Colleges in the United States." *Journal of College Student Retention*, 2002, 4(2), 173–201.

Liu, R., and Liu, E. "Institutional Integration: An Analysis of Tinto's Theory." Paper presented at the annual meeting of the Association for Institutional Research, Cincinnati, Ohio, May 2000.

Metzner, B., and Bean, J. "The Estimation of a Conceptual Model of Nontraditional Undergraduate Student Attrition." *Research in Higher Education*, 1987, 27(1), 15–38.

Murtaugh, P., Burns, L., and Schuster, J. "Predicting the Retention of University Students." *Research in Higher Education*, 1999, 40(3), 355–371.

National Center for Education Statistics. *The Condition of Education 2004*. Washington, D.C.: U.S. Department of Education, 2004.

Pascarella, E. "Student-Faculty Informal Contact and College Outcomes." *Review of Educational Research*, 1980, 50(4), 545–595.

Soldner, L., Lee, Y., and Duby, P. "Welcome to the Block: Developing Freshman Learning Communities That Work." *Journal of College Student Retention*, 1999, 1(2), 115–129.

Tinto, V. "Dropout from Higher Education: A Theoretical Synthesis of Recent Research." *Review of Educational Research*, 1975, 45(1), 89–125.

Tinto, V. "Enhancing Student Persistence: Connecting the Dots." Paper presented at the meeting of the Wisconsin Center for the Advancement of Postsecondary Education, Madison, Wis., October 2002.

TERRY T. ISHITANI *is an assistant professor in the educational research program at the University of Memphis.*

8

This volume presents new approaches to displaying information that can be used in decision making and institutional research.

A Few Concluding Thoughts

Terry T. Ishitani

Institutional researchers face a wide range of challenges in the area of institutional planning, and these challenges are never static. These professionals provide carefully composed data and information to stakeholders at each stage of planning. Since planning is a process, it is not uncommon to find that the output of the initial objective leads to a new challenge. However, despite the varying challenges, all institutional researchers can benefit from learning how data and information are refined and used to answer questions.

The chapter authors offer their unique perspectives on data and information analysis and how their understandings shape their practice of institutional research. As a result, two important themes have emerged: three chapters evolve around the institutional planning framework or case studies, and the others discuss specific techniques used in exploring alternative approaches to issues in institutional planning. In addition, because of the variety of roles these authors play in institutional research, the breadth of the field is carefully represented and illustrated.

Institutional planning consists of a string of ongoing assessment and evaluation projects that form the planning outcome. In Chapter One, Richard A. Voorhees presents an example of one such a planning style: mixed methods. He notes that "the quantitative paradigm helps strategic planners to describe the 'what' in an organization while the qualitative paradigm can answer the 'why.'" Such ongoing assessment and evaluation are conducted in both quantitative and qualitative forms. The relationship between these two different types of approaches is not exclusive but rather complementary.

NEW DIRECTIONS FOR INSTITUTIONAL RESEARCH, no. 137, Spring 2008 © Wiley Periodicals, Inc.
Published online in Wiley InterScience (www.interscience.wiley.com) • DOI: 10.1002/ir.242

Applications of quantitative and qualitative data are also exemplified by Patricia J. McClintock and Kevin J. G. Snider in Chapter Two. They illustrate how both types of data were important to their freshman student recruitment planning, where the data were used sequentially and concurrently. Their work also attests to the evaluation of the process in planning. For instance, information such as how many high school juniors are considering a particular college to attend in two years is alterable. This type of information is sensitive to external influences, such as the application packages high school students receive from other institutions. Thus, it largely depends on how often and when one collects such data. In a similar vein, admitted students do not necessarily enroll. Therefore, to increase the number of students in a freshman cohort, it is important to monitor changes in the status of the pool of admitted students over time instead of focusing on only one portion of the process. Moreover, as a result of monitoring efforts, the final outcome of the recruitment campaign explored in this chapter was improved by making necessary unplanned adjustments to reach recruitment objectives in the case study.

Another roadblock in the planning process is resistance caused by a shift in institutional culture or practice. Some institutional research offices are understaffed yet field requests for data constantly. Granted, some requests are fairly simple and do not require institutional research personnel to create new queries to complete them. When a large selection of intranet-based reporting systems is available, it can provide solutions to reduce reporting loads. In addition, technologically savvy stakeholders may prefer such a self-directed approach for data and information gathering. However, in reality, implementation of Web-based reporting systems may not be as easy as it sounds. Christopher J. Maxwell in Chapter Three addresses issues related to changes in reporting systems. In addition to the technical difficulties he encountered in implementing a new reporting system, he shares the lessons he learned about political barriers. McClintock and Snider in Chapter Two also describe the tremendous resistance they faced from their constituents when they proposed a different way to recruit freshman students. There is no single method to successfully change cultures that exist within institutional units in exchange for gaining efficiency and effectiveness in planning. However, we may be able to validate the benefits of changing paradigms in institutional practice by presenting quantitative information derived from paradigm changes illustrated in Chapters Two and Three.

Using an HTML application, Iryna Y. Johnson in Chapter Four offers technical instruction on how to combine internal and external data for student recruitment purposes. Johnson's effort to develop such an interface indicates changes in portability of data. Transforming complex data into a tool that allows users to explore details as needed is essential for institutional personnel, such as admission counselors who tend to be away from campus for student recruitment. Data interfaces such as the one Johnson created are mobile; they can be used on any desktop or laptop computer, and they are already designed to be efficient for specific purposes. These data interfaces move from a strategic meeting on campus to a high school counselor's office. Furthermore, miscommunication and misunderstanding often occur when traveling institutional personnel and stakeholders on campus are discussing information on different pages of a large summary report. Thus, creative ways to enhance portability of data is expected to grow as we work to widen data accessibility in institutional research practice.

Data and information need to empower stakeholders in their decision making and policymaking. However, it is a great challenge for institutional research professionals to identify how to compile and present data and information to stakeholders in the most effective manner. This challenge is often heightened when data requests from stakeholders are ambiguous or impossible to gather. In many occasions, stakeholders ask institutional research personnel for data while they are still pondering what they would like to gain from such data. A lack of clear objectives leads to submitting the data, which tend to contain information that may be short of practical utility in decision making. Douglas K. Anderson, Bridgett J. Milner, and Chris J. Foley in Chapter Five have experienced such a dilemma in data reporting and suggest techniques to convert increasingly complex data into more meaningful information for stakeholders. They refer to such data as "actionable information," which is tailored toward stimulating decision makers' thinking. It is becoming more common for institutional researchers to have not only a high level of technical skills for data reporting, but also the ability to refine information for stakeholders. In order to improve data refinement skills among institutional research personnel, working closely with the stakeholder in the planning is crucial.

Efforts in converting data to actionable information that Anderson, Milner, and Foley discuss range from populating data in various formats to developing real-time interactive programs. Similar to the interactive program illustrated in Chapter Five, interactive programs included in Chapters Six and Seven also serve as a bridge between in-depth statistical analyses and practical application of results from such analyses. Due to rapid advances in computing technologies, cutting-edge statistical techniques such as Bayesian modeling and event history modeling can be applied in the area of institutional research. Using such analytical approaches, we can examine existing issues in higher education from different angles. In Chapter Six, Yonghong Jade Xu and I describe how Carnegie Classification places institutions into certain institutional categories using Bayesian modeling. Our chief objective in the chapter is to suggest an analytical approach for exploring classification methods when such methods are rather unknown to the public. Given the fact that many institutional stakeholders are sensitive to annually published college rankings, Bayesian modeling shows its potential in investigating college-ranking methods. Results from these studies may yield significant implications for institutional characteristics where institutions can focus on improving their standing in the rankings.

In Chapter Seven, I shift my approach to college attrition from explanation of attrition to prediction of departure. Event history modeling allows institutional researchers to identify students at risk of departure and to assess the timing of their departure. Knowing students are at risk of departure at certain times can help identify needed changes in retention efforts at the institutional level. Constituents and practitioners involved in intervention programs to facilitate student retention can target students at risk and intensify their intervention based on the timing of their departure. However, researchers and stakeholders are often disconnected due to the fact that researchers fail to offer tools to stimulate stakeholders' thinking based on study findings. Based on my experience as an institutional researcher, discussion using interactive programs such as those illustrated in Chapters Six and Seven tends to be more dynamic and fast-paced than oral or written research reports. I believe that such programs will be widely developed in the future as our creativity in institutional research continues to expand.

TERRY T. ISHITANI is an assistant professor in the educational research program at the University of Memphis.

NEW DIRECTIONS FOR INSTITUTIONAL RESEARCH • DOI: 10.1002/ir

INDEX

Note: f indicates figures, t indicates tables.

IR133 **Using Quantitative Data to Answer Critical Questions**
Frances K. Stage
This volume of *New Directions for Institutional Research* challenges
quantitative researchers to become more critical. By providing examples
from the work of several prominent researchers, and by offering concrete
recommendations, the editor and authors deliver messages that are likely to
cause many educational researchers to reexamine their own work. The
collective efforts described here will help readers become more sensitive to
the nuances among various educational groups, and to pay more attention to
outliers. This volume supplies both motivation and analytical support to
those who might incorporate criticality into their own quantitative work, as
well as to those who wish to read critical perspectives with an open mind
about what they might find.
ISBN: 978-07879-97786

IR132 **Applying Economics to Institutional Research**
Robert K. Toutkoushian, Michael B. Paulsen
In many ways, economic concepts, models, and methods can be applied to
higher education research. This volume's chapter authors are all higher
education researchers with graduate training in economics and extensive
experience in institutional research. They share insight on the economist's
perspective of education costs and revenues, plus how to use economics to
inform enrollment management and to understand faculty labor market
issues.
ISBN: 978-07879-95768

IR131 **Data Mining in Action: Case Studies of Enrollment Management**
Jing Luan, Chun-Mei Zhao
Data mining has great potential to enhance institutional research. Six case
studies in this volume employed data mining for solving real-world problems in enrollment yield, retention, transfer-outs, utilization of advanced-
placement scores, predicting graduation rates, and more. Discusses data
mining vs. traditional statistics, debunks the myths, and highlights the need
for individual pattern recognition and customized treatment of students.
ISBN: 0-7879-9426-X

IR130 **Reframing Persistence Research to Improve Academic Success**
Edward P. St. John, Michael Wilkerson
This volume proposes and tests new collaborations between institutional
researchers and others on campus who are engaged in breaking down
barriers to academic success, especially for minorities and nontraditional
students. What if traditional recommendations aren't effective? Chapters
review prior research and best practices, then investigate new approaches to
assessment, action research, action inquiry, and evaluation. Lessons learned
can inform strategies of administrators, faculty, and everyone interested in
improving success for all students.
ISBN: 0-7879-8759-X

IR129 **Analyzing Faculty Work and Rewards: Using Boyer's Four Domains of
Scholarship**
John M. Braxton
Boyer's four domains—scholarships of discovery, application, integration, and
teaching—influence and define scholars as their professional roles, career
stages, and research goals change. This volume offers practical suggestions for
academic reward structure, graduate school preparation, and state policy.
ISBN: 0-7879-8674-7

IR128   **Workforce Development and Higher Education: A Strategic Role for Institutional Research**
Richard A. Voorhees, Lee Harvey
Workforce development is a growing area for higher education. This volume examines its conceptual underpinnings from an international perspective, and it provides practical institutional case studies and specific techniques for gauging the market potential for new instructional programs. It discusses suggested projects and studies for IR personnel to consider on their campuses.
ISBN: 0-7879-8365-9

IR127   **Survey Research: Emerging Issues**
Paul D. Umbach
Demands for accountability are forcing colleges and universities to conduct more high-quality surveys to gauge institutional effectiveness. New technologies are improving survey implementation as well as researchers' ability to effectively analyze data. This volume examines these emerging issues in a rapidly changing environment and highlights lessons learned from past research.
ISBN: 0-7879-8329-2

IR126   **Enhancing Alumni Research: European and American Perspectives**
David J. Weerts, Javier Vidal
The increasing globalization of higher education has made it easy to compare problems, goals, and tools associated with conducting alumni research worldwide. This research is also being used to learn about the impact, purposes, and successes of higher education. This volume will help institutional leaders use alumni research to respond to the increasing demands of state officials, accrediting agencies, employers, prospective students, parents, and the general public.
ISBN: 0-7879-8228-8

IR125   **Minority Retention: What Works?**
Gerald H. Gaither
Examines some of the best policies, practices, and procedures to achieve greater diversity and access, while controlling costs and maintaining quality. Looks at institutions that are majority-serving, tribal, Hispanic-serving, and historically black. Emphasizes that the key to retention is in the professional commitment of faculty and staff to student-centered efforts, and includes practical ideas adaptable to different institutional goals.
ISBN: 0-7879-7974-0

IR124   **Unique Campus Contexts: Insights for Research and Assessment**
Jason E. Lane, M. Christopher Brown II
Summarizes what we know about professional schools, transnational campuses, proprietary schools, religious institutions, and corporate universities. As more students take advantage of these specialized educational environments, conducting meaningful research becomes a challenge. The authors argue for the importance of educational context and debunk the one-size-fits-all approach to assessment, evaluation, and research. Effective institutional measures of inquiry, benchmarks, and indicators must be congruent with the mission, population, and function of each unique campus context.
ISBN: 0-7879-7973-2

IR123   **Successful Strategic Planning**
Michael J. Dooris, John M. Kelley, James F. Trainer
Explains the value of strategic planning in higher education to improve conditions and meet missions (hiring better faculty, recruiting stronger students, upgrading facilities, improving programs, acquiring resources), and

what planning tools and methodologies have been used at various campuses. Goes beyond the activity of planning to investigate successful ways to implement and infuse strategic plans throughout the organization. Case studies from various campuses show different ways to achieve success.
ISBN: 0-7879-7792-6

IR122 **Assessing Character Outcomes in College**
Jon C. Dalton, Terrence R. Russell, Sally Kline
Examines several perspectives on the role of higher education in developing students' character, and illustrates approaches to defining and assessing character outcomes. Moral, civic, ethical, and spiritual development are key aspects of students' growth and experience in college, so how can educators encourage good values and assess their impact?
ISBN: 0-7879-7791-8

IR121 **Overcoming Survey Research Problems**
Stephen R. Porter
As demand for survey research has increased, survey response rates have decreased. This volume examines an array of survey research problems and best practices, from both the literature and field practitioners, to provide solutions to increase response rates while controlling costs. Discusses administering longitudinal studies, doing surveys on sensitive topics such as student drug and alcohol use, and using new technologies for survey administration.
ISBN: 0-7879-7477-3

IR120 **Using Geographic Information Systems in Institutional Research**
Daniel Teodorescu
Exploring the potential of geographic information systems (GIS) applications in higher education administration, this issue introduces IR professionals and campus administrators to a powerful presentation and analysis tool. Chapters explore the benefits of working with the spatial component of data in recruitment, admissions, facilities, alumni development, and other areas, with examples of actual GIS applications from several higher education institutions.
ISBN: 0-7879-7281-9

IR119 **Maximizing Revenue in Higher Education**
F. King Alexander, Ronald G. Ehrenberg
This volume presents edited versions of some of the best articles from a forum on institutional revenue generation sponsored by the Cornell Higher Education Research Institute. The chapters provide different perspectives on revenue generation and how institutions are struggling to find an appropriate balance between meeting public expectations and maximizing private market forces. The insights provided about options and alternatives will enable campus leaders, institutional researchers, and policymakers to better understand evolving patterns in public and private revenue reliance.
ISBN: 0-7879-7221-5

IR118 **Studying Diverse Institutions: Contexts, Challenges, and Considerations**
M. Christopher Brown II, Jason E. Lane
This volume examines the contextual and methodological issues pertaining to studying diverse institutions (including women's colleges, tribal colleges, and military academies), and provides effective and useful approaches for higher education administrators, institutional researchers and planners, policymakers, and faculty seeking to better understand students in postsecondary education. It also offers guidelines to asking the right research questions, employing the appropriate research design and methods, and analyzing the data with respect to the unique institutional contexts.
ISBN: 0-7879-6990-7

NEW DIRECTIONS FOR INSTITUTIONAL RESEARCH
Order Form
SUBSCRIPTIONS AND SINGLE ISSUES

DISCOUNTED BACK ISSUES:

Use this form to receive **20% off** all back issues of New Directions for Institutional Research. All single issues priced at **$23.20** (normally $29.00)

TITLE	ISSUE NO.	ISBN
_____	_____	_____
_____	_____	_____
_____	_____	_____

Call 888-378-2537 or see mailing instructions below. When calling, mention the promotional code, JB7ND, to receive your discount.

SUBSCRIPTIONS: *(1 year, 4 issues)*

☐ New Order   ☐ Renewal

U.S.	☐ Individual: $80	☐ Institutional: $185
Canada/Mexico	☐ Individual: $80	☐ Institutional: $225
All Others	☐ Individual: $104	☐ Institutional: $269

Call 888-378-2537 or see mailing and pricing instructions below. Online subscriptions are available at www.interscience.wiley.com.

Copy or detach page and send to:
John Wiley & Sons, Journals Dept, 5th Floor
989 Market Street, San Francisco, CA 94103-1741

Order Form can also be faxed to: 888-481-2665

Issue/Subscription Amount: $ _____	**SHIPPING CHARGES:**
Shipping Amount: $ _____	SURFACE Domestic Canadian
(for single issues only—subscription prices include shipping)	First Item $5.00 $6.00
Total Amount: $ _____	Each Add'l Item $3.00 $1.50

(No sales tax for U.S. subscriptions. Canadian residents, add GST for subscription orders. Individual rate subscriptions must be paid by personal check or credit card. Individual rate subscriptions may not be resold as library copies.)

☐ Payment enclosed (U.S. check or money order only. All payments must be in U.S. dollars.)

☐ VISA ☐ MC ☐ Amex # _____ Exp. Date _____

Card Holder Name _____ Card Issue # _____

Signature_____ Day Phone _____

☐ Bill Me (U.S. institutional orders only. Purchase order required.)

Purchase order # _____
                         Federal Tax ID13559302   **GST 89102 8052**

Name_____

Address _____

Phone _____ E-mail _____